What people are saying about…

IMMOVABLE

Tim Riordan's book, *Immovable: Standing Firm in the Last Days*, is a much needed call to the church to prepare for the days that are ahead. He offers clear Bible teaching on prophecy, relating it to current events, and calls believers to prepare for the spiritual warfare that is to come by showing how the spiritual armor of Ephesians six has special relevance for Christians living in the last days. This book provides a healthy mix of solid biblical teaching and practical life application to help Christians prepare to stand strong in the difficult times leading up to the Rapture and to present a strong witness of the gospel to a world that is in need of salvation. While the days ahead will be challenging, the opportunities to advance the gospel will be unparalleled, and the church must be ready to embrace the challenges and the opportunities. *Immovable* will serve as a useful guide to help Christians stand firm and victorious in the final days before Christ's return.

- Dr. Robert Jeffress, Pastor,
  First Baptist Church, Dallas, Texas

Christ's return is imminent and the church must be prepared. In *Immovable – Standing Firm in the Last Days*, Tim Riordan has challenged believers with anticipated, prophetic events and solid, biblical truth that should awaken the church to the Kingdom opportunities and the spiritual challenges before us. This book will provide direction for the church to put on the spiritual armor of God, to stand firm on the truth of God, and to be vigilant in winning souls for Jesus until He returns. *Immovable* will be a valuable resource for Christians as we make preparations to stand firm in the days ahead.

- Dr. Johnny Hunt, Pastor,
  First Baptist Church of Woodstock, Georgia and former President of the Southern Baptist Convention

One thing is certain about the last days. Christians must know how to stand firm while waiting for Christ to return. Tim Riordan's book, *Immovable*, is a great resource to help believers know how to fight the spiritual battle until Christ comes back. Knowing "how to live" while waiting for Christ to return is a need for every believer and *Immovable* provides very practical help in understanding preparation for the last days.

- Ken Adams, Lead Pastor of Crossroads Church
  Newnan, Georgia

Tim Riordan's book *Immovable: Standing Firm in the Last Days* is a battle cry for believers. We need to hear a clarion call to battle, because we are in a war. Unfortunately, many church folks think the Christian life is a call to board a cruise ship rather than a battleship. Other believers are AWOL and seem to have abandoned the cause of the Kingdom. Riordan's call for us to put on the whole armor of God and stand firm in these last days is timely and powerful. In recent years I have ceased measuring a church's success in terms of attendance, buildings, baptisms and budgets, but in terms of how many people are being prepared for the coming persecution. Riordan's book is reveille for Christians to wake up, stand fast and prepare for the battle.

- Dr. Gerald Harris – Editor, *The Christian Index*

Dr. Tim Riordan pastors a young, growing, contemporary church in the suburbs of metro-Atlanta. He knows first-hand what people are going through on a day-to-day basis, and feels called to minister to them in and with the love of Jesus. As a biblical scholar and student of current world events, however, he also sees difficult days and demanding challenges for Christians and their children looming on the horizon. In his book, *Immovable: Standing Firm in the Last Days,* Dr. Riordan explains in an easy-to-understand fashion his take on Biblical end-time prophecy and makes a strong case for the need for modern-day followers of Christ to be prepared for what is coming. He soberly poses the questions to Christian parents: "Are we training our children to be immovable in the last days before the return of Christ?" Using Paul's letter to the Ephesians, Dr. Riordan explains each part of the "armor of God" and presents it as a workable template for our urgent preparation.

- Dr. J. Wayne Jenkins - Director of Missions
  Western Baptist Association, Newnan, Georgia

Dr. Tim Riordan

IM MOV ABLE

Standing Firm in the Last Days

Dr. Tim Riordan

IM MOV ABLE

Standing Firm in the Last Days

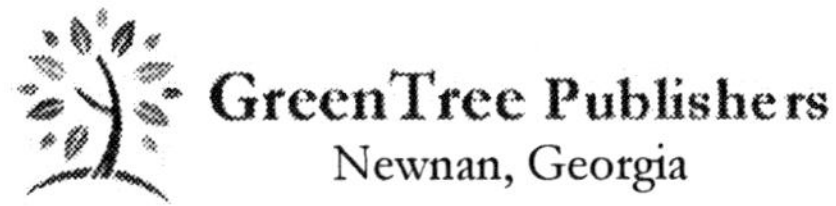

Immovable – Standing Firm in the Last Days

Printed in the United States of America
ISBN-13: 978-0-9909285-0-8 (Greentree Publishers)
ISBN-10: 0990928500

Follow Dr. Tim Riordan through the following media links:
Website/blog: www.timriordan.me
Twitter: @tim_riordan
Facebook: www.facebook.com/pages/Tim-Riordan/
453213784820641

Greentree Publishers
www.greentreepublishers.com

DEDICATION

This book is dedicated to my amazing wife, Sandra: my best friend and partner in life and ministry. The journey is filled with cherished memories, renewing grace, team victories, precious children, and anticipation of the blessings to come.

SPECIAL THANKS...

Ministry is a team sport. This book would have never been a reality if not for the help and support of so many friends. I am so grateful to have a godly family who prays for me, encourages me, and tirelessly reads my manuscripts with great insights and suggestions. I am also thankful for my church family, SonRise Baptist Church in Newnan, Georgia, for your love and encouragement. I also appreciate a number of other friends who gave of their time to read and make suggestions along the way.

Thanks to my assistant, June Black, for her work in helping me with this project, to Carmon Keith for editorial suggestions, to Jenn Riggs who is always so willing to offer her amazing gifts of creativity for my cover design, to Judy Miller for her encouragement and suggestions, and to my editor and friend, Adele Brinkley.

CONTENTS

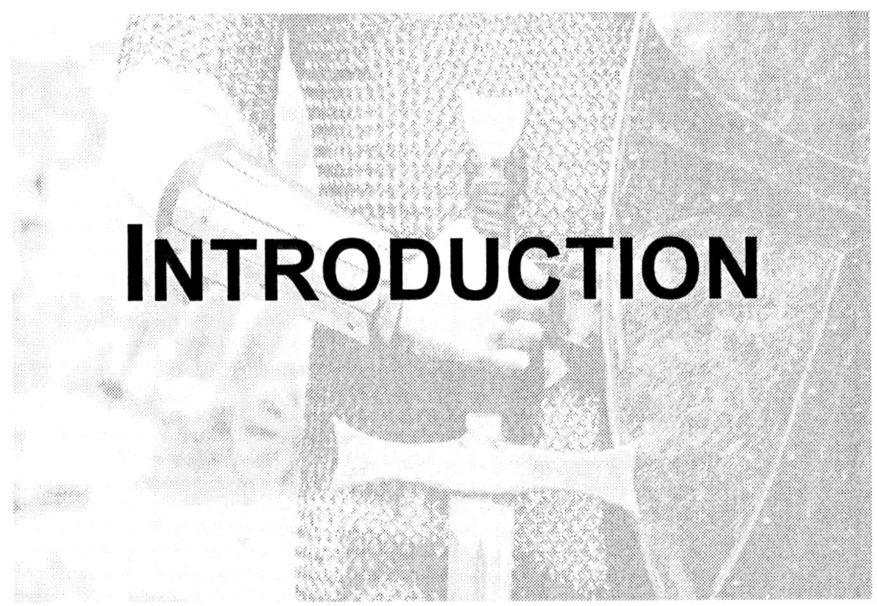

INTRODUCTION

I will never forget standing with a family in a small hospital room, watching the slowing heart monitor hooked to the still, small form of a three-year old boy, who fell into a swimming pool while no one watched. I was supposed to be the spiritual shepherd called to be with a grieving family to provide support, encouragement, and an appropriate word from God. The problem occurred when I walked into the hospital room knowing the boy would soon die. He looked just like *my* three-year old son – tight, curly, blond hair and a tiny, fair-skinned body. If it hadn't been for all the wires attached to this miniature person, he would have looked as if he were taking a nap and would be ready to jump up and run around the room any minute.

In that moment, I was no longer the pastor on call with emotional and spiritual fortitude, the one expected to be the steadfast guide in a tragic moment. I was not the one who, while transparently sharing in the grief with an appropriate emotional response, remained resolute in my ability to lead this grieving family into the open arms of Christ's comfort. Instead, I was the brokenhearted father who looked on the fractured form of his dying son. I became an emotional wreck. As we all huddled around the bed waiting for the heart monitor to flat line, a nurse compassionately placed her hand upon my shoulder comforting me as much as she did the distraught mother.

I learned that day that even in the moments when being immovable is essential, many times it is elusive. It would have been strange, unChristlike, and even inhuman for me not to have been emotionally affected by such an event, but my inability to control my emotions in such a critical time made me less effective at the moment.

People thought Thomas Jonathan Jackson was immovable, and many swore they would follow him to their death. He began his military career in the Mexican-American War but gained his fame as he served under General Robert E. Lee during the Battle of Bull Run in the Civil War. As the Union Army pressed upon the Confederates, Jackson pushed his men to fill the gap and stand firm against the enemy. When Brigadier General Barnard Bee looked back to see Jackson holding fast as the enemy poured toward him, he said to his men, "Look men, there is Jackson standing like a stone wall!"[1] From that day forward, Colonel Thomas Jonathan Jackson became known simply as "Stonewall Jackson." A fierce fighter, immovable in battle, he eventually became one of the best known and most effective generals who led the Confederate States Army.[2] It is unfortunate his reputation of fierceness and immovability in life is tainted by the way he died: accidentally shot by friendly fire and eventually succumbing to pneumonia. Stonewall Jackson earned his nickname, but as history reveals, he was not immovable as he died prematurely from such a senseless accident.

Immovable! Can we comprehend such a concept? When have you needed to be immovable but were unable to find the strength? It may have been an intense spiritual conflict that called for deep, godly strength or a strong temptation in which you needed to put your foot down and say no. Maybe your moment of need came in the midst of a major emotional struggle when you really needed to be strong. Can we stand immovable in critical times?

Perhaps we have to move to the realm of fantasy to find someone who is immovable. You may think of Superman as immovable, but he couldn't handle Kryptonite. While Batman always seems to get out of tight spots, I wouldn't call him "immovable." Is being immovable an illusion, or could it be a reality for us? The answer comes when we consider that which threatens our ability to stand firm. Blogger Jim Loy posed an interesting question: "What happens when an irresistible force meets an immovable object?"[3] If an object, or a person, is immovable, then an irresistible force does not exist. Conversely, if an irresistible force does exist, then immovable objects do not. One will negate the other. We all have experienced forces in our lives that seem to overwhelm and challenge us, but did we stand immovable against them?

The Bible is clear that as time draws to a close, the world will move into a state of chaos and upheaval, presenting various forces that may at first seem irresistible. I do not mean irresistible as in something we absolutely must have, like a piece of my grandmother's chocolate cake. I mean irresistible in a way that no matter what we do to overcome a particular challenge, we cannot win and remain unable to resist or overcome the challenge. Past generations have faced significant challenges, but these challenges pale in comparison to the difficulties that will come.

I am not a doom-and-gloom kind of guy, but in various places in the Bible, God does give us a glimpse into coming events that are indeed quite gloomy. We call these futuristic passages "prophecy," statements made under the inspiration of God about events that will come to pass. God must want us to glimpse often because nearly thirty percent of the Bible is made up of prophecy.[4] Some were made thousands of years ago about future events, but from a twenty-first century perspective, those events are now history, like the birthplace of the Messiah (Micah 5:1-2) or the cruel punishment and death Jesus would endure (Isaiah 53). Jesus fulfilled more than 300 prophetic passages related to His first coming.[5] If God was wrong regarding any of these prophecies, then the whole Bible would be suspect. Because God was 100 percent right about Christ's first coming, we can be confident about His prophecies related to Christ's second coming.

The Bible has much to say about what will be happening in the world when Jesus comes back for the second time.[6] Today, many people are asking questions about current events and wondering if these events point to Christ's imminent return. Others are clueless about current events and how they may relate to Bible prophecy. This lack of understanding may stem from not knowing what the Bible says about the last days. Bible literacy is at an all-time low in our country, so it should not be a surprise that the average person is not tuned in to potential prophetic events as they unfold before our eyes.[7] Others do not seem to care, for they have been lulled into apathy and have already fallen prey to the deception of our age. Some of the chaos and trouble in our own country and in countries around the world could very well be a warning that the trumpet sound calling the church to meet Jesus is soon forthcoming.

When I say "the church," I am not referring to a particular church building in any community, but rather I am speaking of every Christian in the world who has surrendered to Jesus Christ as Lord and Savior. When people become Christians, they immediately become part of the universal church. Bible prophecies about events that will take place during the final seven years of time are horrific. Cataclysmic events will bring such mayhem, pain, and heartache that many people will not be able to endure the struggle, but some Bible scholars think the church will not have to endure the events of this final period of time. The Bible teaches that the church will be raptured at some point before the end of time as we know it. While there is disagreement by Bible students as to the exact timing of the rapture of the church, most Christians agree that the Bible teaches of the church being caught up to meet the Lord. The word "rapture" is not in the Bible, but the concept of being "caught up" to meet the Lord in the air is clearly spoken about in passages such as 1 Thessalonians 4:16-18. Some scholars believe this rapture will happen before the Tribulation Period begins while others believe the church will have to experience a portion of the final seven-year period. Still others think the rapture will happen at Christ's second coming. Whether you believe the rapture will come before the Tribulation, in the middle, or at some other time, there is no doubt day-to-day challenges will get exceedingly worse before the church is taken away to meet the Lord in the air.

As I look at Christians today, I wonder if we are ready for the days ahead. Are we ready to stand firm in these last days leading up to the rapture of the church? Are our children prepared to endure the trials and challenges that are sure to come as the Antichrist prepares to step up onto the world's stage?

This book is written as a guide to help Christians prepare for the days ahead. It is divided into two parts. The first part offers biblical teaching about the last days and compares this teaching to current events indicating we may indeed be the last generation. If we are not the last generation before the return of Christ, then our children or grandchildren could be. Many wonderful books go into great detail about Bible prophecy and current events, and it is not my intent to provide an exhaustive list of every prophecy connected to the current events of our time; however, it is my purpose to provide just enough biblical information and facts about current events for us to consider the possibility that the last days may be upon us.

The second section focuses on the spiritual armor God has provided for the times of spiritual conflict the church will be forced to undergo. While you may have already studied the spiritual armor referred to in Ephesians 6:10-18, I will challenge you to look at it anew as equipment God has given the church so we can stand immovable in the last days leading up to the rapture. The final chapter will offer practical application of the principles outlined in previous chapters. It does not matter what your denominational affiliation may be; God has a message for all of us, and there are things we must do if we are going to engage our enemy with steadfastness.

As you read thoughtfully and prayerfully through these chapters, keep your Bible close at hand and search through additional scripture as God prompts. Talk with your Christian friends about these concepts and study them together. A small group discussion guide is included in the appendices for these times of group study. Preparing to stand firm in the last days is serious business, and we must treat it as such by making it a priority. While Stonewall Jackson was not immovable on the battlefield, he was immovable in his faith. Even though everything about his philosophy and beliefs was not right and his position on slavery was wrong, he was a Christ follower who believed in the Word of God. We, too, can be a stone wall in the face of the enemy, and we must stand with the rest of the church against a resistible force through the immeasurable power of our immovable Lord.

PART I

The Last Days

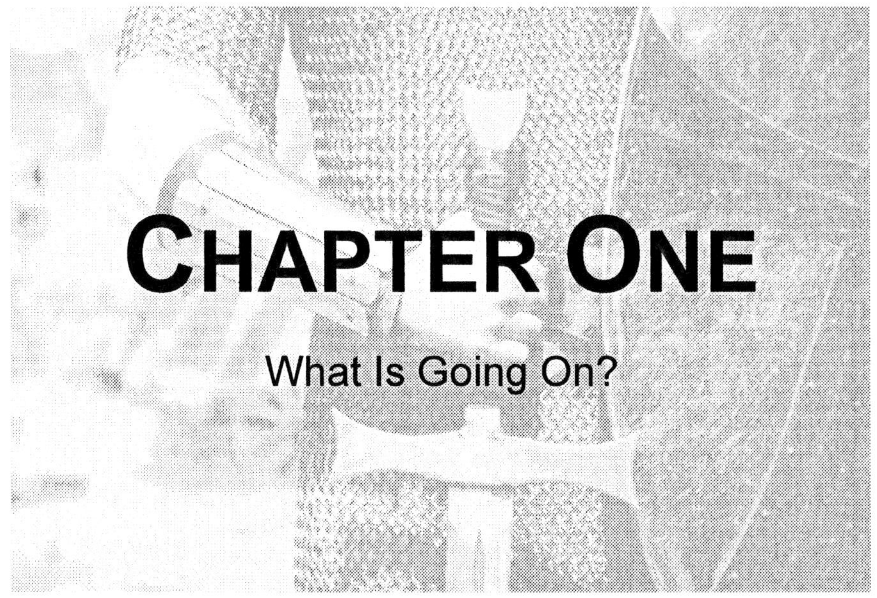

CHAPTER ONE

What Is Going On?

Unless you have purposely tuned out all media, you must admit that current events border on weird. At one time in my life, I could count on world events being somewhat predictable, but those days are gone. In recent years, the United States of America has begun to slide out of control down a slope that will lead to scary and significant consequences, and the rest of the world seems to be enduring additional disconcerting changes. I cite a few examples about which I have read or heard in recent months underscoring that the paradigm of "normalcy" is shifting. I am confident this list could be expanded almost every day as more and more strange events are happening all around us. Regardless of when you may be reading this, I encourage you to reflect upon the current events underscoring the uncertainty of our age.

- A petition from citizens of the state of Texas, with more than 125,000 signatures, was presented to President Barak Obama via the administration's "We the People" website requesting permission for the state of Texas to secede from the United States of America. Texans expressed their disappointment with the federal government's neglect to reform spending and believed their rights and liberties were in jeopardy. Texas is not the only state wanting to secede from the Union. In November 2012, CBS News began an article about this topic with these words:

> They don't want to take their country back. They just want to leave it behind. As the dust settles in the wake of President Obama's decisive reelection last Tuesday, the White House petition website has been flooded by a series of secession requests, with malcontents from New Jersey to North Dakota submitting petitions to allow their states to withdraw from the union.[1]

While these requests began on Election Day, November 6, 2012, by November 14, the number of signatures had grown to 675,000 nationwide with representatives from all 50 states participating.[2] This issue became so prominent that President Obama raised the number from 25,000 to 100,000 needed signatures before the White House would give an official response to a request. As you probably know, our President has not agreed to any state seceding from the Union.

- Earthquakes and natural disasters continue to increase creating additional global instability. While the earthquake in Haiti on January 12, 2010 ranks as number 352 on the scale of the most intense earthquakes in all of history, the number of deaths ranks it in the top five earthquakes in the last 500 years.[3] Who could forget the earthquake and tsunami in Japan in 2011 or Sumatra in 2004? Dr. Saeed Mirza, emeritus professor at Montreal's McGill University, was interviewed about the weak Canadian infrastructure, and he made this astounding statement that would be applicable anywhere in the world: "The frequency and intensity of these events has been increasing at an escalating rate and what was a one in 100 year event at one time may become the norm."[4]

- The recent discussion about gun control was once again sparked by violence in which twenty-six people lost their lives at the hands of a mentally and emotionally disturbed man at Sandy Hook Elementary School in Newtown, Connecticut. On December 14, 2012, a gunman opened fire killing twenty young children and six adults before he turned the gun on himself. In response to this tragic event, commentators throughout America referred to the gunman as being "evil." It is intriguing to hear secular commentators, many of whom do not believe in God, use that term. As a Christian, I know beyond a doubt that evil exists in the world because of sin, but our secular society has spent many years working to relegate truth to the realm of relative as opposed to absolute. If truth is relative, then an event or person cannot be called evil. I wonder if the liberal news agencies thought of that entanglement before writing their reports.
- The moral decline of our nation is indescribable. Our children are watching demonstrations of outright filth on television during prime time, such as a recent MTV Video Music Awards performance that created a stir across the country.[5] Homosexual marriages are gaining widespread acceptance across the country, and twenty-nine states (and Washington D.C.) have now legalized same-sex marriages.[6] On August 29, 2013, the Treasury Department and the Internal Revenue Service announced "same-sex couples who are legally married will be recognized as such for federal tax purposes, even if the state where they live does not recognize their union."[7]
- Not only is the mistrust of government becoming normal in our society, but fear is becoming commonplace everywhere. Because of our government's threat to ban weapons and the threat of violence in America, the sale of firearms has skyrocketed. The Associated Press reported that law enforcement personnel are facing a shortage of assault weap-

ons and ammunition because of a surge in gun sales.[8] One police officer in my home town told me they were months behind on receiving their ammunition order because of unforeseen shortages.

- Would you have ever imagined a city going bankrupt? How about a country? Both have happened, to some extent, in the recent past. While Detroit, Michigan and Greece make strange bedfellows, they share a similar economic struggle. The root cause is quite different, I am sure, but the resulting struggle is quite similar. Greece's troubles were not only expressed in their economic woes, but also in the response of its angry citizens. The Guardian wrote about the instability and chaos the country was experiencing: "Teetering on the edge of economic collapse, Greece is also on the brink of becoming ungovernable; its politicians panic-stricken and discredited; its institutions barely functioning; its people ground down by waves of budget cuts."[9]
- For the first time in the history of our country, American citizens are leaving the country in record numbers.[10] Whereas the United States of America was once the envy of the world with people risking their lives to get in, now there is a new twist. U. S. citizens are also leaving the country in droves. Some of the reasons are economic while others are political. Regardless, the number has increased in recent years. A 2008 study revealed that about three million people each year leave the United States to move to other countries. Since that time, the number has increased.[11]
- Russia is once again rising to global prominence under the leadership of Vladimir Putin. Putin stepped in to broker a temporary resolution with Syria, and the Russian leadership has led soldiers across the Ukrainian borders inciting unrest and political division in an already unstable nation.

- What about the four blood moons? This idea has been in the news often, particularly in response to such noted Christian leaders as Pastor John Hagee and Pastor Mark Biltz. Four lunar eclipses will occur between Passover of 2014 and Sukkoth (the Feast of Tabernacles) of 2015. The interesting thing is that these "blood moons" will happen on four Jewish festivals. Some think this is a sign from God that something significant is about to happen in the nation of Israel, which will affect the whole world.

I could continue to list intriguing and shocking facts that lead us once again to ask, "What is going on?" In my list above, I did not address the alarming financial decisions being made by our political leaders, nor did I touch on the precarious nature of our foreign affairs as evidenced by the murders of U. S. diplomats and workers at an embassy in Libya. I have not mentioned the IRS scandal or the NSA abuse of the privacy laws, and I did not address the problems in the European Union, the political struggles in Egypt, or the civil war in Syria. The list could go on and on.

America was in financial trouble years ago because of our national debt, but in September 2012, our debt surpassed the $16 trillion mark. According to Congressman John Boehner, this means every American adult and child would have to pay more than $50,000 to pay off our national debt. We pay more than $370 billion a year in interest as a nation, more than twice what we have spent on education in our country and one-third the amount being spent by the Defense Department.[12]

While the intent of this book is not political, I cite these events and issues to point out that something is amiss. Many others are also asking questions about the current state of our nation. In a 2008 NBC/Wall Street Journal poll, 73 percent of Americans thought the United States was in a state of decline.[13] On December 27, 2012, the *Star Ledger* in New Jersey declared, "What we are witnessing today may be remembered as the early stages of America's decline. If you put aside national pride for a moment and take an honest inventory, that sobering conclusion is hard to avoid."[14] While many of these illustrations relate to the United States of America, we could easily see that unrest and political disturbances exist globally.

Current Events and a New Reality

While not everyone is in agreement regarding the current condition of the United States, many are looking unfavorably at our circumstances. Some are predicting a robust comeback, but others are saying too much is stacked against us to be able to come out unscathed. A lot of people are wondering where these circumstances will lead and how we should respond to them. If it were just contained to the United States, we would be justifiably concerned, but some of the problems are being felt worldwide, making our concerns even greater. The *International Forecaster* reported, "Perhaps with the exception of Germany, the world economy is in disarray. Every major economy otherwise is in trouble in one way or another."[15] While this particular article focuses on the economic woes of our global community, the upheaval of Syria, the bombing of another embassy on September 11, 2012, and the continuing struggles of the European Union are just a few indications that problems are being experienced on a global scale.

What do all of these reports mean? Two possible solutions can be considered. While I struggle to see the validity of this first option, it could mean we are going through a global correction, and we will come out on the other side in better condition than we were before the slide began. Indeed, some optimists believe we will pull out of this nosedive and find greener pastures. For example, the *St. Louis Post-Dispatch* wrote an article about former Vice-President Al Gore's outlook and gave it the title "As World Spins Faster Toward Trouble, Gore Claims Optimism."[16] I would like to have confidence in this perspective, especially for the sake of my children and their future children, but I cannot justify this position while also considering the teaching of Scripture.

The second possibility, and in my opinion the most probable, is that our world will never return to "the way it used to be." I am not suggesting that we will never find solid ground again, but I am proposing that our new reality will require significant adjustments. Based upon my studies of Scripture, I believe we are moving quickly toward the return of Christ. While I will explore this in more detail in the following chapters, I address a concept Jesus presented to us as He talked with His disciples on the Mount of Olives, located just across the Kidron Valley from Jerusalem.

Jesus' Warnings of Last Days Trends

In Matthew 24:4-8, Jesus' disciples asked what signs they could anticipate that would let them know He was about to return. Jesus answered their question by giving us the longest prophetic teaching about His return:

> Watch out that no one deceives you. For many will come in my name, claiming, 'I am the Messiah,' and will deceive many. You will hear of wars and rumors of wars, but see to it that you are not alarmed. Such things must happen, but the end is still to come. Nation will rise against nation, and kingdom against kingdom. There will be famines and earthquakes in various places. All these are the beginning of birth pains. (NIV)

Focus for a moment on Christ's last words in this passage. While the first four things Jesus mentioned are signs of His second coming, He called these "the beginning of birth pains." While it is difficult for me to speak about birth pains, I have observed them on six occasions as I coached my wife through the births of our six wonderful children. I would like to share a few observations from these experiences.

- *Birth pains start gently and gradually increase in intensity.* One of the first things you learn how to do in childbirth classes is to count. I know we learned that in kindergarten, but labor room counting is kindergarten math under duress. You start out counting with a clock as you time the distance between the start of one contraction to the start of another. Mild contractions mark the beginning of birth pains weeks before the mother goes into labor. They start out easy and eventually grow so intense that the laboring mother feels as if she may not be able to stand it. For Jesus to say these events are the beginning of birth pains, He is pointing out that these cataclysmic events will start gently and grow in intensity.

Before His return, the world will exist in such chaos and pain that many will not be able to stand it. I believe there will be untold suicides as a result of the unbearable hopelessness by those left to go through this time. It is because of the concept of increased intensity that I tend to lean toward the view that the way things used to be will never be again. Why? Because we are seeing signs of Christ's return all around us, and as Christ's return draws closer, these signs will grow in intensity. I also believe Scripture points out there will be a one-world government during the Tribulation Period, and for a one-world government to be instituted, it must be preceded by global chaos and a worldwide failure. A world leader, which the Bible calls the Antichrist, will rise out of this turmoil to lead the world to some level of stability thereby gaining world recognition and trust.[17]

- *The beginning of birth pains can easily be misconstrued.* Every mother has learned by experience the difference between Braxton Hicks contractions and active labor. WebMD calls Braxton Hicks "false labor" and says "They are your body's way of getting ready for the 'real thing.'"[18] Starting during the mother's second trimester, false labor is merely a tightening of the abdomen causing mild, irregular pains that are more localized. By contrast, active labor is much more intense with pains that are consistent and wide spread. During false labor, a mother is aware of the pain, but she is able to carry on her normal, daily routine, whereas active labor is disabling. In the same way, the events we have seen on the news over the past years have certainly been noticeable discomforts in the wellness climate of our world but not painful enough to disable us. We have recognized these irregular pains but carry on with our daily routines. Could it be that these events are "the beginning of birth pains?" Is it possible that these false labor pains have been going on for years and have been spoken of in Bible prophecy centuries ago?

- *Birth pains change the nature of the mother.* I've seen my sweet, compassionate, petite wife become another woman just hours before the birth of our children. It is true that she is a real champion, and I marvel at her inner strength, but it is also true that this kind of pain affects one's personality–at least temporarily. As our nation begins to go through these biblical birth pains, we will see adjustments that cause us to change almost overnight. For example, laws maintaining our revered privacy are now being ignored and groups who pose threats to a particular political agenda become targeted by federal agencies. New laws passed and regulations will be imposed in response to what is going on in the world. These things will lead to greater instability, thereby setting the stage for the Antichrist to make his grand appearance.

I return to my original question: What is going on? I think the stage *is* being set. The score has been written, the conductor is picking up his baton, and the symphony is about to begin. This symphony, however, will be nothing like works written by Beethoven or Mozart. The experience will come across as a chaotic modern orchestral piece emitting a cacophony of disturbing sounds leading to heartache and confusion. I am saying the final act may very well be about to begin.

While the Bible says no one can predict when the "last days" will officially begin (Mark 13:32), we do know Christians will be living in the world until the moment the church is raptured. Regardless of our position about the time the church is raptured or the Second Coming of Jesus, Christians need to be prepared for the last days leading up to the rapture and ultimately to the end of the age. If we are the generation who will be alive at the return of Christ, we must be prepared. If it is not this generation, it could be our children's or our grandchildren's generation. What will you do to be ready?

CHAPTER TWO

Are We Living in the Last Days?

"Are we there yet?" is a familiar question coming from any young child while on a long trip, and it's a good one. It comes from one who is tired of the journey and ready for the destination. Many today are wondering the same thing regarding the last days, or at least we want to know "How much farther?" We, too, are tired of the journey, and our destination offers us eternal relief from the growing struggles we face in this day. We long for the journey to be complete. Some people are asking the question simply out of curiosity, while others are confronting current events and the prospects of the last days with great fear. Regardless of the reasons, many people have begun to see a correlation between prophetic teaching about the last days and current events. Are we living in the last days?

It's really not a bad question or even one that is out of the ordinary. We all like to know the length of a journey before we ever begin. I usually Google information about a trip before I leave home so I can determine the distance and projected arrival time, and then I periodically check my iPhone for updates on my progress toward my destination. The older I get, the more I realize the reality of the words to the old Gospel song: "This world is not my home. I'm just passing through."[1] Because I'm just passing through, my destination is obviously somewhere beyond this world: Heaven. The Bible teaches there is one of two ways for me to arrive at my final destination. I may die a physical death, immediately leave my body, and move to my new home in Heaven. The principle in God's word is "to be absent from the body is to be present with the Lord" (2 Corinthians 5:8). The other option is that I may be one of those who are still alive at the time when Jesus returns to take His church home. So the question becomes, "When will Christ return?" Is the clock of time as we know it winding down? Is it possible that we will be alive when the trumpet sounds and Jesus returns for His bride, the church?

What are the Last Days?

Are we there yet? First, we must explore what is meant by the "last days?" Apocalyptic talk these days contains all manner of religious overtones, but what does this talk really mean? My position comes from a biblical world view and is not affected by what the Mayans believed or what Nostradamus predicted. *Baker Encyclopedia of the Bible* says the last days are "the final period of the world as we now know it."[2] Terms the Bible uses to describe this time period include "last days" (2 Peter 3:3), "latter days" (Daniel 2:28: NIV translates it as "days to come"), "last times" (1 Peter 1:20), and the "last hour" (1 John 2:18). The "last days" describes a period of time that concludes with the Second Coming of Jesus Christ. His return is described as "the day of the Lord" (2 Peter 3:10), "the great and terrible day of the Lord" (Malachi 4:5), "the day of judgment" (1 John 4:17), and "great day of God Almighty" (Revelation 16:14). While this day will not literally mark the last day of the world's existence, it does mark the end of a significant chapter in God's unfolding history. Christ will return, Satan will be defeated, and Christ's millennial reign will begin.

While there are varying opinions about the timing of the Second Coming of Jesus, I place it and the rapture of the Church at two separate times. The Bible says there will be a time when Jesus meets believers in the air and takes them home with Him to Heaven (1 Thessalonians 4:16-18). The word "rapture" communicates the idea of being "caught up" to meet the Lord and has become a common word in the Church to describe this significant prophetic event that Christians anticipate. The Second Coming of Christ is distinguished from the rapture in that Jesus actually comes to the earth. The Second Coming will take place at the end of a period of seven years called the Tribulation Period. It is not the intention of this book to go into detail about these two prophetic events, other than to say they are going to happen. One could relegate the concept of "last days" to describe the months leading up to what the Bible calls the Battle of Armageddon or even to the seven-year Tribulation Period; however, I choose to use the term "last days" to refer to the time leading up to the rapture of the Church and the seven year Tribulation Period.

When will Jesus Return?

Jesus indicated signs of His return, and His teaching is cited in three of the Gospels (Matthew 24, Mark 13, and Luke 21). While there are some excellent books that go into great detail about these signs, I will mention them only briefly later. Consider the commentary Jesus gave on the list of signs. Days before Christ's crucifixion, His disciples asked Him, "What will be the sign of your coming and of the end of the age?" (Matthew 24:3). It is important to note that Jesus gave signs of the end of the *age*, which will happen after the seven years of the Tribulation Period. In the middle of His list of signs, Jesus said, "All these are the beginning of birth pains" (Matthew 24:8). While these events will take place before Christ's return, they will begin long before the actual Day of the Lord, as noted in the previous chapter. As we consider our current time, we need to study the list of the "signs" and ask ourselves if we are seeing evidence of these prophecies. Beginning in Luke 12:54, Jesus criticized His contemporaries for not being aware of the signs of His first appearance, so it seems logical that Jesus would expect us to take His list of signs for His second return and be keenly aware of our times.

Are we living in the last days? The short answer is only God knows, but there is strong evidence to support the opinion that we could be. I must be quick to point out the error of some who have tried to pinpoint a day and even an hour of Christ's return for His church. While predictions of Christ's return may seem to be a recent declaration, they are not something new:

- In the second century, Montanus, a self-proclaimed prophet, told followers the New Jerusalem was coming down from Heaven on Asia Minor. Many followers abandoned possessions and broke family ties to prepare for the event.
- William Miller, founder of Adventism in America, calculated the return of Christ to be October 22, 1843. His followers sat dressed in white on hills and housetops waiting for the end of the age.
- Former NASA engineer and Bible student, Edgar Whisenant published a book that gained national recognition: *Why the Rapture Will Be in 1988*. He predicted it would happen during Rosh Hashanah (September 11-13, 1988). When the rapture didn't happen, he moved it up a year and wrote a new book: *89 Reasons the Rapture Will Be in 1989*. While his first book was a best seller, I am certain the second did not go over as well.
- Harold Camping predicted the return of Christ would take place on September 7, 1994. On his radio broadcast, he claimed to be "more than 99% certain" his prediction was accurate. Because his first prediction did not come to pass, years later he predicted the rapture would happen on May 21, 2011, and the end of the world would come on October 21, 2011. Once the rapture didn't take place on his specified day,

he said it was a silent judgment and the world would still end on October 21. When October 21st past and was uneventful, he retired from broadcasting and stepped down from Family Radio.

A car magnet on a vehicle in a local Wal-Mart parking lot declared Christ's return to be September 18, 2012. I wonder what the owner of the car did with the magnet on the 19th.

Many people have made startling predictions regarding Christ's second coming and the end of the world, but none were accurate. Were these people serious? Yes. Were they sincere? Yes, but sincerely wrong. The Bible is clear no one will know the date of Christ's return: "No one knows about that day or hour, not even the angels in heaven, nor the Son, but only the Father. Be on guard! Be alert! You do not know when that time will come" (Mark 13:32-33).

One problem with such blatant claims from well-meaning, sincere Bible teachers is that many people are lulled into complacency or disbelief. People have a tendency to write off such modern-day prophets declaring them to be fanatics and therefore ignore the reality of Christ's promised return. For Christians, these types of claims bring surprise and ultimately embarrassment when they do not come to pass. This embarrassment eventually leads us to be hesitant to talk about the imminence of Christ's return. Somehow we must not allow some Bible teacher's misplaced enthusiasm to cause us to ignore one of the most life-altering truths in the Bible for Christians.

While Jesus did tell us that no one will know the day or hour, He did say for us to "be on guard," and to "be alert." In other words, just because some misplaced predictions have received a lot of press, do not ignore the fact that He is coming again. There will be a significant number of Christians living in the days leading up to Christ's return. While every Christian in every generation ought to live every day as if it were his or her last, true last days Christians will be greatly affected by the circumstances leading up to the end of the world as we know it. We must, therefore, be ready.

What does the Bible say about Today's News?

Several key clues presented by Old Testament prophets help us to evaluate the daily current events we read about online or hear reported on the news. The prophecies in the Old Testament had an immediate partial fulfillment at times, while other instances the full completion spoken of by the prophet would take place sometime in the future. Other prophecies have a specific fulfillment that must take place sometime in the future with no immediate application. Let's consider some of those prophecies.

Daniel

The Old Testament book of Daniel usually leads us to think about lions and fiery furnaces, but Daniel provides us some key indications about the last days that must be considered if we are going to be prepared for what will ultimately take place. In the second chapter, King Nebuchadnezzar had an important dream, and God gave Daniel the interpretation. Daniel concluded his interpretation in verse forty-five with this statement: "The great God has shown the king what will take place in the future." God presented to us through Nebuchadnezzar's dream a brief foretelling of the future of the world. In this dream, the king saw a statue.

> The head of the statue was made of pure gold, its chest and arms of silver, its belly and thighs of bronze, its legs of iron, its feet partly of iron and partly of baked clay. While you were watching, a rock was cut out, but not by human hands. It struck the statue on its feet of iron and clay and smashed them. Then the iron, the clay, the bronze, the silver and the gold were broken to pieces at the same time and became like chaff on a threshing floor in the summer. The wind swept them away without leaving a trace. But the rock that struck the statue became a huge mountain and filled the whole earth. (Daniel 2:32-35)

According to Daniel's interpretation (Daniel 2:36-45), the statue represented the four main powers in the history of the world. The golden head represented Nebuchadnezzar's kingdom of the Babylonians. The chest and arms of silver represented the Medo-Persian Empire that began with the conquering of Babylon in 539 BC and lasted for about another 200 years. Daniel referred to this dual monarchy in a prophetic way in Daniel 5:28 and made it clear to Nebuchadnezzar that his kingdom would be given to the Medes and the Persians.

The next section of the statue was the "belly and thighs of bronze." With a view of history, you can see this part represented the next world power of the Greeks under Phillip of Macedon and his son, Alexander the Great. Daniel plainly acknowledged Greece would be this world power (Daniel 8:21). The final part of the statue above the feet was the "legs of iron." Though Daniel did not mention the name of the next world power, we know the two legs represented the coming Roman Empire. There seems little doubt by Bible scholars this part of the statue spoke of the two political areas of the Empire: the Latin-speaking west with the capital in Rome and the Greek-speaking east with the capital in Constantinople. Since the Roman Empire, there have been several military or political leaders who have tried to conquer the world (Genghis Khan, Napoleon, Adolf Hitler, etc.), but each was unable to do so.

The statue's feet represented one final world power that is still to come. We know this is futuristic because there has been no world kingdom since the Roman Empire. It is to be a future Roman Empire with a division of ten kingdoms or distinct leaders. In this interpretation, Daniel indicated this last league of kingdoms will be on the earth when God sets up His earthly Kingdom, thus predicting the state of world affairs in the last days.

Daniel had another dream years later about a ten-horned beast that corroborated Nebuchadnezzar's dream and expanded upon this prophecy (Daniel 7). The ten horns represented the ten rulers who oversaw the ten divisions mentioned previously. One of the rulers rises above the others and becomes the dominant world dictator. This final kingdom is a picture of a one-world government made up of ten leaders, or one could assume, ten regions. In some ways, it is difficult to imagine a one-world government, but in another way it is not. Just in my lifetime, I have seen the financial market move from being national to global. There was a time that you could invest in a particular company that was listed for national stock exchange on NASDAQ, and the increase in the value of the stock was limited to whatever that company did in our country. Such national influence has changed, for we have seen companies spreading their business to other countries. Little by little, the global market has changed. What happens in the Japanese market (NIKKEI) has a huge impact on what will happen in the United States market. We are now realizing that our economic success is closely tied to the economic success of Great Britain, Japan, China, and other countries.

While the concept of a one-world government may seem farfetched to us, it has been the topic of numerous discussions from world leaders for many years.

- After World War I, Woodrow Wilson sought to establish the League of Nations, which many saw as a first step toward a one-world government. It was formed as a part of the Versailles Treaty in 1919. Historian Rebecca Gruver highlighted the purpose of the treaty: "In calling for the League, the president sought to replace power politics with a worldwide alliance to maintain an orderly, peaceful world."[3] President Wilson believed strongly that the League of Nations would prevent the occurrence of another world war. A Council was established within the League that was empowered to use force against a nation that broke the peace agreement. In other words, the League was a global police force intended to ensure conformity by the Central Powers to the guidelines of the treaty.

- President Wilson's closest advisor, Colonel Mandell House, and others founded the Council on Foreign Relations (CFR). This council was actually born out of the Presidents "think tank" that was tasked with the challenge of helping Wilson prepare for peace talks and develop a strategy for a postwar peace. The CFR eventually evolved from this group and has consistently promoted a one-world government since its inception. One proposal coming from this group that was discussed by our Congress was the possibility of removing our northern and southern borders and thinking more like North Americans instead of just Americans. "On Capitol Hill, testimony [was heard] for Americans to start thinking like citizens of North America and treat the U.S., Mexico and Canada like one big country." [4]
- The CFR was the primary group that established the United Nations in 1945, which has provided a forum for world leadership since its inception. The CFR has presented options through the United Nations (UN) for a global police force and an instrument through which global policy can be developed.
- An organization called the "Club of Rome" was founded in 1968 at David Rockefeller's estate in Bellagio, Italy. The group describes itself as "addressing the root causes of the challenges and crises the world faces today."[5] It consists of current and former Heads of State, United Nations bureaucrats, high-level politicians and government officials, diplomats, scientists, economists, and business leaders from around the globe. "The Club of Rome acts as a platform which brings together academics, scientists, politicians, business professionals and members of the civil society to design, develop and implement effective approaches on a broad range of interconnected global issues."[6] According to *The Green Agenda*, The Club of Rome stated, "We are facing an

imminent catastrophic ecological collapse" and "our only hope is to transform humanity into a global interdependent sustainable society, based on respect and reverence for the Earth."[7] In 1972, the Club of Rome proposed a plan to divide the world into 10 regions, which, of course, is reminiscent of Daniel's vision.[8]

- Some contemporary writers, such as David Jeremiah and Tim LaHaye, have wondered if the European Union (EU) could be a move in this direction. It is interesting to look at a map of the old Roman Empire and compare it to a map of the twenty-nine current EU countries. You cannot help but see the similarities as well as the possibilities of the EU being the new Roman Empire.[9] Regardless of whether it is or not, it is still an interesting consideration.

A one-world government will necessitate a one-world currency. A few years ago it would have been quite difficult to imagine the United States giving up the tried and true dollar bill, but as we watch the dollar's value decline, it is easier to see this as a possibility. There has been a concerted effort to move us toward a global currency in recent years.

- On November 5, 2009, the project-syndicate.org website had the following to say about a global currency: "Globalist billionaire financier George Soros announced to the world that the economy of the United States was about to come to an end. The International Monetary Fund would make the necessary recommendations as to a suitable replacement for the U.S. dollar, which would be some type of international currency." Soros' commentary on *The Japan Times* online expresses similar thoughts.[10] Soros called for the UN and its Security Council to serve as the overseeing enforcement body for this new financial system.
- According to the American Free Press, in 2009, Soros spent $50 million to begin the Institute for New Economic Think-

ing, the purpose for which is to advance the idea that a global government and a global economy are absolutely necessary for our survival.[11]

- On December 8, 2007, it was reported that the Iranian government refused to accept the dollar for payment for oil. Payment now must be made in Euros. Oil Minister Gholam Hossein Nozari labeled the greenback as an "unreliable" currency.[12] Iran continues to counter U. S. sanctions by threatening the U. S. dollar.[13]
- Texas Congressman Ron Paul, who was also a presidential candidate in the 2012 Presidential race, predicted the fall of U. S. dollar and a one-world currency by 2012, though that did not happen.

When you consider these events and reports together, you cannot help but see the form of Daniel's statue taking shape.

Jesus' Teaching

Jesus knew more about His planned return than anyone. The Olivet Discourse, Jesus' teaching in Matthew twenty-four, provides us the greatest information about world events leading up to Christ's Second Coming. As Jesus and His disciples left the temple, the disciples commented to Jesus about the buildings. They were probably referring to the temple's grandeur, but Jesus replied with these words: "Do you see all these things?' he asked. 'Truly, I tell you, not one stone here will be left on another; everyone will be thrown down.'" You can imagine these words created quite a stir among Christ's little group of insiders. They wanted to know more about these events, so when they sat down on the Mount of Olives, they said to Jesus, "Tell us, when will this happen, and what will be the sign of Your coming and of the end of the age?" (Matthew 24:3). The question the disciples asked was two-fold: "When will this happen?" and "What will be the sign of Your coming and of the end of the age?" The "this" in the first question appeared to relate to the destruction of the temple, which happened in A.D. 70. Jesus' focus on the second question related to His return and the end of the age. In an effort to answer these questions, Jesus gave to his followers a list of signs that included deception, wars, famines, earthquakes, persecution and international hatred of Christians, apostasy, betrayal, false prophets, spiritual apathy, proliferation of the gospel, "abomination that causes desolation," great distress, miracles leading to deception, disturbance in the heavens, and the sign of the Son of Man. As we consider the hour at hand, a few in-depth observations are needed.

Great Deception

Jesus warned of deception six times in this teaching. In Matthew 24:4-5, Jesus warned His disciples, "Watch out that no one deceives you. For many will come in my name, claiming, 'I am the Christ,' and will deceive many." One only needs to reflect on the last few years to see this has already happened. Consider the following:

- 1993: The Branch Davidians in Texas were led by David Koresh, a self-proclaimed messiah of sorts.
- 1997: Heaven's Gate was a UFO cult led by Marshall Applewhite in California. Applewhite led his followers to believe they needed to commit mass suicide so their souls could unite with a UFO hidden behind the Hale-Bopp comet and travel through space.[14]
- A 2007 CNN report told of Jose Luis de Jesus Miranda: "The minister has the number 666 tattooed on his arm. But Jose Luis de Jesus Miranda is not your typical minister. De Jesus, or 'Daddy' as his thousands of followers call him, does not merely pray to God: He says he is God."[15]
- A 1997 *Time Magazine* article addressed the move toward spiritual mysticism as the 20th century drew to a close: "These are the waning years of the 20th century, and out on the margins of spiritual life there's a strange phosphorescence. As

predicted, the approach of the year 2000 is coaxing all the crazed out of the woodwork. They bring with them a twitchy hybrid of spirituality and pop obsession, part Christian, part Asian mystic, part Gnostic, part X Files...we have seen the Beast of the Apocalypse. It's Bambi in a tunic."[16]

- We have moved from easy "believism" to outright heresy. In our spiritual-experience seeking society, we need not necessarily have a Christ-figure to emerge with some new truth. Numerous popular preachers today preach a message of easy believism where Christianity does not necessarily call us to repent from our sin but rather to look to God for happiness and provision. In most cases, the message of the Christian pop-culture is not just an omission of biblical teachings but rather reflects an anti-biblical stance. Should we be surprised? The Apostle Paul warned Timothy. "For the time will come when men will not put up with sound doctrine. Instead, to suit their own desires, they will gather around them a great number of teachers to say what their itching ears want to hear. They will turn their ears away from the truth and turn aside to myths" (2 Timothy 4:3-4).

Wars and Rumors of Wars

Jesus warned the disciples there would be much fighting between nations as the end drew near. In Matthew 24:6-7, He said, "You will hear of wars and rumors of wars, but see to it that you are not alarmed. Such things must happen, but the end is still to come. Nation will rise against nation, and kingdom against kingdom." One could say this prophecy could apply to any generation, and certainly this statement is true. There have been approximately 15,000 wars in recorded human history. As the calendar rolled over to the twenty-first century, we found ourselves at a standoff with Iraq over nuclear weapons that ultimately

Famine and Earthquakes

Jesus also predicted great calamity around the world from what seems to be natural disasters. "There will be famines and earthquakes in various places. All these are the beginning of birth pains" (Matthew 24:7-8). Pictures of starving children displayed for the world to see have been commonplace during my adult life as famines and pestilence around the world have become familiar themes. Tim LaHaye and Jerry Jenkins discussed the rise of earthquakes in our world:

> During the period from 2000 to 2008, the total number of earthquakes worldwide each year that were recorded with a magnitude of 3.0 to 3.9 increased from 4,827 to an astonishing 11,735. Likewise, those with a magnitude of 4.0 to 4.9 increased in number from 8,008 in the year 2000 to 12,291 in 2008 while those measuring 5.0 to 5.9 rose from 1,344 to 1,768 ... The rise of earthquakes in recent times has been so dramatic (and so time-consuming for those whose job it is to record the data), that the USGS National Earthquake Information Center decided in 2009 to discontinue its practice of keeping records of earthquakes that were smaller than a magnitude of 4.5, unless those earthquakes resulted in fatalities or significant damage.[18]

Though earthquakes have not maintained this trend in the years following 2008, the abundance of these natural disasters along with the deaths and destruction they have caused keeps this prophecy before our eyes.[19] I think it will be valuable to view the increase of natural disasters from a thirty-year or fifty-year perspective, and we will no doubt become more aware of the increased activity.

Proliferation of the Gospel

I have been a witness to the growing reality that Jesus' prophecy in Matthew 24:14 will be fulfilled in my lifetime: "And this gospel of the kingdom will be preached in the whole world as a testimony to all nations, and then the end will come." Wycliffe translators report that "today, portions or the entire Bible have been translated into over 2,300 languages and dialects covering over 90% of the world's population...Bible societies distribute approximately 600 million Scripture portions or entire Bibles every single year."[20] Countdown.org reports, "The gospel has been preached to over four billion people in the world. Over fifty million Bibles are distributed every year, as well as nearly eighty million New Testaments. Four billion gospel tracts are also printed each year."[21] It is easy to see how the Internet is one tool that will help make this prophecy a reality. People all over the world have access to the worldwide web, thereby making Bible teachings available with the stroke of a key. Another evidence that has created anticipation of this prophecy being fulfilled in my lifetime is the emphasis by numerous organizations upon reaching the unreached people groups of the world. For example, one of the key focuses of the largest Protestant denomination in the world, the Southern Baptist Convention, is leading churches to adopt unreached people groups and work to plant multiplying churches among these communities all over the world.

Gathering of the Jews in Israel

One prophecy that seems to have started the "last days buzz" was the fulfillment of Ezekiel 37:21-23 where Israel became a nation and Jews returned to Israel:

> This is what the Sovereign Lord says: I will take the Israelites out of the nations where they have gone. I will gather them from all around and bring them back into their own land. I will make them one nation in the land, on the mountains of Israel. There will be one king over all of them and they will never again be two nations or be divided into two kingdoms. They will no longer defile themselves with their idols and vile images or with any of

> their offenses, for I will save them from all their sinful backsliding, and I will cleanse them. They will be my people, and I will be their God.

This passage does indicate a spiritual revival among the Jews, and we have seen many Jews coming to Christ in recent decades. The number of Jewish people living in Palestine has grown from 25,000 in 1917, when the Balfour Declaration was signed at the end of World War I, to nearly seven million today.

Many other prophecies could be considered, but these discussed in this section lead us to consider the possibilities of the times. We could be living in the last days, or they could be coming soon! While it is unbiblical to try to pinpoint a date and time of Christ's return, we are wise to be alert to the times and aware of our current events.

Chapter Three

Preparing for Battle

I have been a student of current events ever since I had to turn in a current event report in ninth grade. Over the years, my interest has changed from a school assignment to general curiosity to serious attentiveness as I have started to connect the dots of events on the world stage to statements of prophecy in the Bible. As a child, I heard of prophecy conferences that were held in meeting rooms at local hotels. At that time, I perceived those speakers to be fortune tellers who would come to town with their charts and illustrations predicting the end of the world. Looking back, it seems these individuals were written off by most mainline Christians as eccentric fanatics who could find symbolism in every nuance of the Bible and fulfilled prophecy in every tree that bloomed. I'm not so sure now that these teachers were so fanatical or eccentric. They may not have been completely right with their pronouncements or theologically sound in their interpretations, but they did believe the Word of God was being lived out before their very eyes and published in the morning paper.

The "last days" theme is becoming more and more common in contemporary writing. For example, New York Times bestselling author, Joel C. Rosenberg, has written extensively connecting current events to Bible prophecy.

> I believe we are [living in the last days]. After decades of studying Bible prophecy, reading hundreds of books on these subjects, discussing prophecy with many Bible teachers and scholars in the U.S. and around the world, analyzing geopolitical events, global economic trends, and spiritual and cultural trends, and seeing so many prophetic signs come to pass, I have come to the conclusion that the Rapture of the church is increasingly close at hand... While all the signs of the last days have to happen before the second coming of Christ, no sign of the last days has to happen before the Rapture occurs.[1]

John MacArthur continues the theme of the imminent return of Jesus when he said, "Christ could come at any moment. I believe that with all my heart – not because of what I read in the newspapers, but because of what I read in Scripture."[2] While authors such as MacArthur and Rosenberg believe Christ's return could be any day, Jesus gave a general command regarding the church and the end of time in Mark 13:33 when He said, "Be on guard! Be alert! You do not know when that time will come." This is a command to be aware of the times and anticipate Christ's return. While we cannot know for certain when Christ is returning, some key signs indicate His return is near. Earlier I listed a few signs of which Jesus spoke and mentioned there were other signs of Christ's return in the Bible. One fulfilled prophecy that began to move us toward the final chapter of history was the rebirth of Israel.

The Rebirth of Israel

Israel ceased being a self-governing nation in 586 B.C. Though Cyrus of Persia allowed the Jews to return to Jerusalem in 539 B.C. (see Ezra 1:1-4), they never enjoyed total sovereignty again. From 167-63 B.C., they did experience some political and religious freedom under the leadership of the Maccabees. Even this period of partial freedom was squelched when Rome became the world power, thereby making Israel once again a subservient state to the empire. In 70 A.D., Rome destroyed Jerusalem, thus relegating the Jewish people to the pages of ancient history – or so the rest of the world thought.

The prophet Isaiah predicted a rebirth of this nation in Isaiah 66:8: "Who has ever heard of such a thing? Who has ever seen such things? Can a country be born in a day or a nation be brought forth in a moment? Yet no sooner is Zion in labor than she gives birth to her children." This did indeed happen on May 14, 1948, and our own President Truman had a significant role in bringing it to pass. While a number of events led up to Israel's newly declared sovereignty, the announcement of their rebirth by the United Nations did seem to come suddenly. With this rise of a Jewish state, ancient tensions began to simmer in the Middle East thereby setting the stage for yet another biblical prophecy.

The Rise of Islam and Islamic Hostilities

The tension between the Arabs and the Jews is as old as the sibling rivalry between Isaac and Ishmael (see Genesis 21:8-14). While there are no prophecies that specifically point to a rise of Islamic hostilities in the last days, there are other predictions that require a strong alliance against Israel. Ezekiel spoke of a five-nation alliance with Russia that would attack Israel. Through God's Holy Spirit, Ezekiel even named these countries, using ancient names of early history (see Ezekiel 38:5-6). We can look at the location of these ancient civilizations and determine their contemporary counterpart. We know without doubt that Iran and Libya will be a part of this group along with Ethiopia/Sudan. The final two members of the alliance are a little more difficult to distinguish with certainty, but many think them to be Germany and Turkey. Scripture does point out that "many nations" will join in this alliance. If one looks at the members of this group and considers current world tension, one could easily see a coalition of Arabic nations banding together to attack their age-old enemy, Israel.

Over the years, some type of coalition has been formed between Russia and these five nations. Search the Internet on recent alliances between Russia and each nation, and you will encounter solid relationships that have recently been formed. The only nation that did not establish such an alliance with Russia is the Sudan/Ethiopia region, but leaders of this region recently established a military agreement with Iran, which is of course, one of the members of the coalition. While I do not believe these countries are warming up their jet engines and setting their sights for Israel just yet, this type of camaraderie certainly sets the stage for some future attack.

An attack on Israel in the last days (the Battle of Gog and Magog) is one in which Israel will stand alone against this alliance (read more about this battle in Chapter Eight). No other nation will come to her defense. You might wonder about the relationship Israel has with the United States. Where will the United Nations be during this attack? Ezekiel once again predicts that other world powers will slap Russia's hand for such hostilities, but no one will militarily come to Israel's defense. Prophecy points to the fact that before this attack can happen, the alliance between the United States and Israel, as well as other countries, will need to be weakened. We only need to be a little aware of current events to see that such changes appear to be happening before our eyes. We would not have been able to imagine the United States breaking our alliance with Israel a few years ago; however, recently, our commitment has certainly changed. While our alliance is still in place, many Americans are concerned about its weakened state. A number of circumstances could be underscored as evidence of this policy change, but one recent piece is the repeated expressions of disfavor toward Israel's threat of a preemptive strike on Iran. Not only have some political analysts in our country come to this conclusion, the Iranian Supreme Leader Ali Khamenei expressed his view of the United States' weakening relationship with Israel in an Iranian newspaper: "With diminishing support for Israel and with the (upcoming) collapse of the monarchy in Saudi Arabia, there won't be any obstacles left facing Iran with its policy of annihilation of Israel."[3]

The Real Battlefield

With all this talk of war, the title of this chapter seems to clearly call us to get ready for military maneuvers, yet this is not the battle I'm talking about. The wars and rumors of wars will simply be a wakeup call to remind us that we might be living in the last days. They are also reminders to us that a greater war is going on all around us that does not involve bombs and missiles. The Apostle Paul wrote to the church in Ephesus giving them instructions on how to live the Christian life. In the last section of his letter, beginning in chapter six, Paul gave the early church instructions on how to understand the spiritual battle. He gave them, and us, specific instructions on how to fight this battle by putting on spiritual armor. The concept of "spiritual warfare" can be a little disturbing to some people, and others write off as eccentric those who speak of this kind of warfare.

Such concepts are not true as it relates to spiritual warfare. The Bible speaks of our current spiritual battle, and God actually uses images of warfare to describe Christians in their daily lives. Consider the Apostle Paul's comment to the church at Philippi when he called Epaphroditus a "fellow soldier" in Philippians 2:25. Philemon was also instructed to view Archippus as a "fellow soldier" in verse two of Paul's letter to Philemon. Timothy was told to "endure hardship with us like a good soldier of Jesus Christ" (see 2 Timothy 2:3). When Paul was coming to the end of his life, he told Timothy that he had "fought the good fight" (see 2 Timothy 4:7). 2 Corinthians 10:3-5 contains a vivid description of our charge to engage the enemy in spiritual warfare:

> For though we live in the world, we do not wage war as the world does. The weapons we fight with are not the weapons of the world. On the contrary, they have divine power to demolish strongholds. We demolish arguments and every pretension that sets itself up against the knowledge of God, and we take captive every thought to make it obedient to Christ.

While I have an adverse reaction to fanaticism and extreme emotionalism when it comes to spiritual warfare, the fact remains that God speaks of it as though it should be an expected and active part of our lives. In the following chapter, I will address some warnings regarding a consideration of spiritual warfare, but in the meantime, we must acknowledge it is a reality for every believer.

Returning to Paul's comments about spiritual warfare found in Ephesians 6:10-13, he presents an interesting relevancy to the study on last days:

> Finally, be strong in the Lord and in the strength of His might. Put on the full armor of God, so that you will be able to stand firm against the schemes of the devil. For our struggle is not against flesh and blood, but against the rulers, against the powers, against the world forces of this darkness, against the spiritual forces of wickedness in the heavenly places. Therefore, take up the full armor of God, so that you will be able to resist in the evil day, and having done everything, to stand firm.

It seems that when Paul wrote, "so that you will be able to resist in the evil day, and having done everything, to stand firm" (verse 13), he was referring to a specific time and not just to general spiritual challenges in the Christian life. While "the day of evil" can refer to a time of intense temptation or spiritual conflict that can come at any point in any Christian's life, it seems that God may be calling us to think about THE day of evil. Is it possible that this passage is calling Christians approaching the last days to prepare for battle by putting on spiritual armor? Certainly, the principles would apply to any kind of spiritual challenge, but can we think of a greater spiritual battle than that which Christians will face in the days and months leading up to the rapture of the church? I do not want to be dogmatic here and say this passage is definitely about the last days, but I certainly think there is some strong teaching here about preparing to stand during the times of greatest spiritual challenge.

The Church's Greatest Challenge

Let's focus on this passage with new eyes and see specifically some things God may be telling us to do in preparation for the most challenging experience in the life and history of the church: the last days. This section begins with a strong command that we must consider carefully and be reminded about the necessity of knowing our orders. Verse ten says, "Finally, be strong in the Lord and in the strength of His might." In the verses leading up to this section on spiritual warfare, Paul has instructed Christians on how to apply the principles of God to their daily lives. He has discussed how being filled with the Spirit affects our marriages, our families, and even our relationships with our employers (owners in the first century world). It's almost as if he takes a breath and says, "Finally." He has one final bit of application that seems to be the peak of the crescendo. He is about to share some important insight about winning the spiritual battle, and success will have nothing to do with our strength. It has everything to do with God's strength.

Look carefully at the command "be strong." In the language of the New Testament, it is a present, passive, imperative verb. Consider the ramifications of this grammar. Because it is present tense, it denotes continuous action. In other words, God is saying we must keep on being strong every moment of every day. He wasn't just saying be strong on a certain day at a certain time, but rather God is telling His children to continue to be strong every moment as we face the evil one. Continuous strength is critical because Satan never attacks at a convenient time. He carefully schemes and finds our moment of greatest weakness. These human tendencies explain why God tells us to continuously be strong. We cannot afford to have a lax moment where our guard is down, for, it is in that exact moment Satan will launch his attack. As the church moves into the challenges of last-days living, it is critical that believers always stand in God's strength as the enemy of our souls will always be looking for opportunities to wreak havoc in our lives.

The second part of this Greek verb is the voice: passive. As a passive verb, it denotes we are recipients of action or we are acted upon. In other words, we are not really the ones doing the "being." Our strength does not necessarily come because we spend hours in our spiritual gym getting our bodies and minds ready to face the enemy. Do not misunderstand me. There are other places in Scripture where we are told to discipline ourselves and prepare ourselves mentally and spiritually for the challenges we are certain to face. Consider 1 Timothy 4:7: "Have nothing to do with godless myths and old wives' tales; rather, train yourself to be godly." Certainly, being godly would have a significant impact on defeating the enemy. It might be important to note, as John Ortberg emphasized in *The Life You've Always Wanted*, God doesn't just tell us to *try* to be godly, but rather He says we should *train* ourselves to be godly.[4] While Ortberg's emphasis could lead to a whole different discussion on spiritual discipline, suffice it to say God does command us to discipline ourselves spiritually so we can be strong when we face the evil one. With that said, this passage in Ephesians 6:10 is not telling us to practice such self-help in our spiritual conquests. This passage is telling us that any strength we have to face our spiritual battles must come from the Lord. Ephesians 6:10 should be properly translated, "be continually strengthened in the Lord." To translate the Greek word as "be strong" seems to indicate there is something we can do to face the challenges of the evil day, but because it is passive, we realize our role is to yield to the power of Christ in us. It is similar to other passages, such as Philippians 4:13, which tells us our strength is in Christ: "I can do all this through Him who gives me strength."

Because this word is an imperative, being continually strengthened in the power of Christ is not an option. We are commanded to yield to Christ in us as we walk daily in His power. Because of Paul's use of "finally" and because of the drawing conclusion of this letter, there is great passion in Paul's plea and command to be strong. Strength in the Christian life is not an option or a suggestion. God has commanded us, as if our lives depend upon it, to be strong in the Lord.

Equipped for the Challenge

Not only should we know our orders to be strong, we must also know our resources. Ephesians 6:11 says, "Put on the full armor of God, so that you will be able to stand firm against the schemes of the devil." While a significant portion of this book will focus on the spiritual armor, an essential resource for spiritual battle, there are a few preliminary thoughts we must consider about its pieces. For example, while we should mentally know the names of the different pieces of spiritual armor, we must *choose* to put our resources to work. Although we are told to "be strong in the Lord," we are also commanded to "put on the full armor of God." While the English words translating the Greek here look to have a similar feel as the command of verse ten ("Finally, be strong in the Lord"), the Greek is actually different. This word is a command, but it is not an example of passive voice. It is middle voice and, therefore, means the subject, which is the church, is to act consciously and willfully on her own volition. In this case, we are to take the initiative to put on the full armor of God. The idea of putting on armor has the same feel as putting on a coat or work clothes. Paul presented the same concept in Romans 13:12-14:

> The night is nearly over; the day is almost here. So let us put aside the deeds of darkness and put on the armor of light. Let us behave decently, as in the daytime, not in carousing and drunkenness, not in sexual immorality and debauchery, not in dissension and jealousy. Rather, clothe yourselves with the Lord Jesus Christ, and do not think about how to gratify the desires of the flesh.

It is significant that God didn't just say we are to put on the armor of God, but rather we are to put on the *full* armor of God. The command emphasizes that every resource God has provided us for spiritual battle is essential. You can't expect to stand in the evil day by wearing just the helmet of salvation. You must have every piece of armor in place and functioning. Consider first century warfare. No soldier in his right mind would go into battle without every piece of his armor. We, too, must understand the significance of every piece and endeavor to dress daily for the battles we may face.

This passage not only calls us to know our resources and our orders, but we are also to know our enemy. Such knowledge is critical because Satan works hard to cause us to misunderstand who our enemy really is. This misunderstanding is evident in the passion with which Christians engage other Christians in theological debates while their participation in personal evangelism only garners lackluster enthusiasm. It is also seen in attitudes some church members have toward other church members who may disagree with them on a non-critical church decision such as carpet color or worship style or whether or not the church should use artificial flowers in the church lobby. It is also easy to be misled into thinking our spouse is our enemy while struggling with one of a myriad of potential issues creating marital strife. If married couples could come to realize Satan is the enemy of strong marriages, they could pursue conflict resolution as a spiritual battle where the host of hell is the enemy and one's spouse is his or her spiritual teammate.

Know the Enemy

In our focal passage, the Apostle Paul presents our objective, or at least one of them, as being able to stand against the devil's schemes (Ephesians 6:11). He goes on to say in verse 12, "For our struggle is not against flesh and blood, but against the rulers, against the powers, against the world forces of this darkness, against the spiritual *forces* of wickedness in the heavenly *places*." It is clear that regardless of how we feel toward a hostile neighbor or a political party, people are not our enemy. He says we do not wrestle against "flesh and blood." It is true that sometimes it seems our battles are against people, but this passage reminds us there is more to the story. We all have experiences with this, but a personal one comes to my mind that God often uses to help me maintain an eternal perspective.

I once had a neighbor who presented quite a challenge. He would complain about the craziest things. My oldest daughter had her wedding in our pasture, and 30 minutes before the wedding, my neighbor drove his truck over to the fence separating our property and proceeded to present me with a list of gripes containing language that was quite offensive. I have heard that pastors are not supposed to get ticked off, so I will just say I was significantly "grieved in my spirit." I imagined all manner of things happening to my neighbor, including trees falling on him, lightning bolts coming from heaven, and someone mysteriously slashing his tires. Needless to say, my spirit was far from right. This event led to other ridiculous claims and accusations toward me that were becoming quite frustrating, and one night he came to my home to attack me verbally. I was not home, so he shared a few strong words with my wife. When my sweet wife called to explain that she had been disrespected by this man, a line had been crossed. It was time for some righteous indignation.

I do not recall ever being so angry as I drove home that night. When I got home, I discovered my youngest daughter was still up waiting on me. Mary Kathryn was six years old at the time, and the events of the night had greatly disturbed her. My anger was quite obvious to anyone within a 10-mile radius, but my young daughter simply replied, "Daddy, he just needs Jesus." It was like the Lord hit me with a wooden post to knock some spiritual sense into my head. While I was not wrong to come to the defense of my wife, I did need to be reminded of the real issue at hand. Even though it may always seem like it, we are not wrestling or struggling with flesh and blood. *People are not our enemy.*

Because the verse states we are not wrestling with people, it insinuates we ARE wrestling with spiritual forces. The word translated wrestling or struggling describes what soldiers would do in hand-to-hand combat. Though I've never been in the military, I imagine firing a missile at the enemy would be stressful, but hand-to-hand combat would be incredibly intense. Hand-to-hand combat is a life or death experience. The stakes are high. The effort is strenuous. The struggle is intense. There are things going on in a spiritual realm that are even more intense than the apparent circumstances. A war is being waged for my neighbor's soul, and it took the perspective of my sensitive daughter to help me see that my enemy is not my neighbor.

This passage also points out that our enemy is multifaceted. We are fighting against "rulers, authorities, powers of this dark world, and spiritual forces of evil." I want to hasten to say that while Scripture does show us the enemy of our souls is challenging, strong, and complex, we do not really know everything about spiritual warfare. I will discuss this lack of understanding further in another chapter, but for now, we need to accept the fact that we cannot fully grasp everything about how the battle is waged against us. We must be careful and not create methods of the enemy the Bible does not specifically describe. I've heard too many strange battle tactics from creative and imaginative people who have no biblical basis. For example, I heard of one spiritual warfare "expert" who said because Satan is the prince of the power of the air, we must pray against him from the highest places in the city, such as a tall building, if we want to gain the spiritual upper hand. I do not believe the Bible is saying your altitude will determine your spiritual fortitude! I think it is safe to say we do not know every detail about the war being waged in the spiritual realm, but we are definitely part of it.

We do know that Satan is powerful and not one to be engaged without great spiritual preparation. We also know that Satan is not omnipresent; therefore, he does his destructive work with the help of a multitude of demons. In Luke 8, Jesus sailed across the Sea of Galilee and encountered the Gaderine demoniac. Verse 27 says, "When Jesus stepped ashore, He was met by a demon-possessed man from the town. For a long time this man had not worn clothes or lived in a house, but had lived in the tombs." In the following verses, we learn that he was endowed with supernatural, physical strength. He actually broke the chains people tried to use to constrain him. When the demon-possessed man encountered Jesus, he fell at Jesus' feet in recognition of Christ's lordship. Verse 30 says, "Jesus asked him, 'What is your name?' 'Legion,' he replied, because many demons had gone into him." The Apostle Paul underscores the demonic horde as he alludes to some of the complexity of spiritual battles in 1 Timothy 4:1: "The Spirit clearly says that in later times some will abandon the faith and follow deceiving spirits and things taught by demons."

Because Paul spoke about standing against the devil's schemes, we know that Satan is not only strong, but he is also crafty. The Greek word translated "schemes" means "methods, cunning arts, deceit, craft, or trickery." Satan knows just which button to push and which method to employ to move us closer to defeat. He doesn't come to us looking like the devil with a pitch fork. 2 Corinthians 11:14 says he comes to us disguised as "an angel of light." As a pastor, I've been amazed at the number of people who have justified affairs, theft, and bigotry within their own minds. Satan has fed his followers with enough prompts to lead us to think that homosexuality is an orientation, lying is misspeaking, and adultery is an indiscretion. Because Satan is strong and crafty, God tells us in 1 Peter 5:8, "Be alert and of sober mind. Your enemy, the devil, prowls around like a roaring lion looking for someone to devour." The fact that we need the full armor and not just a few pieces underscores the strength of our enemy. While this concept has been true throughout all of time, we know that during the last days spiritual warfare will get exponentially worse. If there has ever been a time Christians need the full armor of God, it is now. If indeed we are living in a period of time leading up to the last days, Satan's work will begin to intensify. The Bible teaches us that before Christ's return, Christians will be persecuted and ridiculed, truth will be distorted, natural disasters will abound, and wars will escalate.

What God really wants for His church is for us to stand when the evil day comes. In one place, He says He wants you to "stand your ground;" while in other places, He simply says He wants us "to stand." In this introduction to spiritual armor (see Ephesians 6:10-13), God uses the word "stand" repeatedly to describe His objective for us. As the opposite for stand is fall or fail, God wants us to gain spiritual ground in the great spiritual conflict, not lose it. He wants us to withstand temptation to sin and not fall prey to Satan's schemes. If we are going to stand firm in the last days, to be *immovable*, we need to understand this armor and know how to wear it.

CHAPTER FOUR

Dangers to Avoid

In J. R. R. Tolkien's *The Lord of the Rings*, the Hobbits had little concern or awareness about world affairs or the spiritual conflict about them. It seems as if Tolkien created these creatures and their little world in the Shire to represent us in our safe worlds, totally oblivious to the evil lurking around us. Though the Bible speaks about the spiritual battles in our world, it does not go into great detail in helping us understand how these battles are waged. Because of the "other worldness" of this concept, we have a tendency to hide in our own Shires of comfort and oblivion and ignore the reality of evil that abounds. Even when someone speaks of "spiritual warfare," we shrug off the speaker as eccentric or the subject as extreme. Should we have this kind of attitude about such topics?

My first real encounter with the concept of a spiritual battle going on around me came during an experience at youth camp when I was in seventh grade. A group of adults and students came back from a walk along the beach and told of an encounter with a creepy sort of man who appeared to be deranged. As the adults tried to share the gospel with this individual, he became angry and agitated. They were unable to really communicate with the man who ultimately told them he belonged to Satan. They asked the man his name, and he replied, "Legion." He refused to listen to them as they tried to witness to him, and he recoiled at the name of "Jesus." As the man became more and more agitated, he eventually threw himself into the ocean, and "slithered" away. Looking back on this experience now, I realize this could have been someone who was mentally disturbed or an individual trying to scare a group of students, but I also know it could have been true demonic activity. The only problem for me at the time was that it was quite scary, and that experience became my concept of spiritual warfare. My understanding of spiritual warfare was accentuated by additional reading in some of the popular Christian comic books and illustrated tracts that presented demonic activity as "alive and well on planet earth" (to borrow the title of a book I saw as a child).While Satan may well attack at that level today, most of my spiritual battles are not nearly as overt. I am also concerned that movies like *Poltergeist* or extreme stories of demonic activities and exorcisms cause people to write off the concept as something reserved for Hollywood or eccentric tent meetings.

Spiritual Warfare: the Truth

As we begin this discussion, it is critical to underscore the truth that Satan is indeed alive and working in our midst. There is demonic activity going on all around us at a level we cannot even begin to understand. There is too much Scripture describing the spiritual battles for us to ignore their realities. Ephesians 6:12 speaks to this reality quite plainly: "For our struggle is not against flesh and blood, but against the rulers, against the authorities, against the powers of this dark world and against the spiritual forces of evil in the heavenly realms."

While the concept of spiritual warfare has its roots in the pages of Scripture and is certainly presented to us as a current reality, it seemed to grow in popularity during the mid to late 20th century. One can only surmise the reasons for such growth, but I have confidence my thoughts seem solid.

I believe one cause of the growth in popularity of the concept of spiritual warfare came from the growth of the Charismatic movement. This movement is free to explore and to experience the supernatural. In many circles of this group, truth is determined by experience; therefore, supernatural experiences are evaluated and have become the basis for developing a theology of spiritual warfare. I am sure that some of these experiences are valid and give us a clearer understanding of the spiritual battles going on around us, but other experiences may not necessarily be grounded in biblical teaching and might lead followers of that train of thought to create unfounded means of confronting the wicked forces of evil. Truth is not determined by experience but rather by the word of God (I'll write more thoroughly to this topic later). It is possible for us to have an experience and create all manner of interpretations of that experience that would fall into the category of extra-biblical. I think experience should always be interpreted by the truth of Scripture thereby bringing clarity and biblical balance to our experiences. With that said, the Charismatic movement has been a wonderful gift to the evangelical church in that it has brought the reality of spiritual conflict to the forefront of our Christian experience.

Another influence on the church leading us to hear more about spiritual warfare is the role of some church growth experts and schools of ministry and theology. Examples include Fuller Theological Seminary and writers, such as Peter Wagner and Neal T. Anderson. Two particular books written by Wagner have been a significant influence on Christian leaders: *The Third Wave of the Holy Spirit*[1] and *Signs & Wonders Today*.[2] Wagner coined the idea of a third wave while being interviewed by *Pastoral Renewal* magazine to describe a new movement or activity of the Holy Spirit in our day.[3] It does not take much research to learn that God seems to be doing something new and fresh among us as revival is spreading in places in the world that were once recipients of great mission endeavors. Supernatural events are taking place, and people are being saved in large numbers.

I read an amazing story told by missionary Donald Richards. A land owner in South America gave university students the opportunity to care for his land as they studied ecological principles in caring for rain forests. They were responsible for a total of about 200,000 acres. Richards was somehow involved as a mentor to these Christian university students. When the team did research about the location, they discovered the government had determined there to be at least two tribal groups in the area, and no one had ever been granted permission to enter these areas or contact these groups. As the students began working on their ecological plan for this area, they also began praying about reaching these unreached people groups. After driving through the jungles for hours on muddy, rugged roads that were more like paths for jungle creatures, the group eventually came to a village they later learned was the home of the Karitiana people. Though some of the Karitiana spoke some Portuguese because of previous trading trips with the outside world, the students were the first group of outsiders any of the tribesmen had seen in at least ten years.

As the group of students entered the village, they realized everyone was gathered in a central hut having some kind of meeting, and the students were invited to enter the hut. Upon seeing the guests, the man in the middle stopped the meeting and told the group, "This is where we celebrate Jesus." Richards and his fellow Christians knew no one had ever entered this region to evangelize these people, so they were quite shocked to hear this declaration. The man then proceeded to tell them a year earlier he had a vision. Jesus appeared to him and took him to heaven. He said it was amazingly beautiful, but he noticed no Karitiana people lived there. He asked Jesus why none of his people were there. Jesus told him, "Because you are serving demons, not Me." Jesus then told this man He made the Karitiana people and wanted them to worship the one, true God. Through the vision, the man heard enough of the gospel to become a Christian and lead his people to begin following Jesus as well. At the time this story was written by Bob Sjogren and Bill and Amy Stearns, there were 35 Christians among the tribe, which numbered 156.[4]

Though this story is quite fantastic, it is well documented and certainly presents evidence of God working in unusual ways to reach His world. There have been other claims of supernatural events that may not be as clearly documented, and some people may have a difficult time believing the stories. While I might be hard pressed to agree with every belief and position of various Charismatic leaders, I believe that as the end of days draws ever closer, the spiritual battle will be waged with even greater fervor, and the need for active spiritual warfare will increase.

Another significant shaper of thoughts about spiritual warfare is the influence of fictional writings about the topic. For example, Frank Peretti's books, such as *This Present Darkness* and *Piercing the Darkness,* have presented suggestions as to how spiritual warfare might be waged in our world. I say "suggestions" because his descriptions of spiritual warfare do not have total biblical support but rather seek to fill in the gaps created by biblical silence on some of the details of this topic. Whether or not spiritual warfare is waged exactly like that described in some of this literature, the vivid descriptions have, if nothing else, caused many Christians to consider the possibilities and to become aware of the realities of spiritual hosts.

A Hunger for Authenticity

Stirring the hearts and minds of believers as we consider the growing interest in spiritual warfare, there is a hunger for an experience in the spiritual realm that moves one beyond the repetitive tradition and anticipated experience of typical church life. Christians in every age group are coming to the conclusion that there is more to Christianity than a sleepy service on Sunday and a lazy attempt to follow the Ten Commandments throughout the week. A deep yearning moves in the hearts of many Christians to experience God in His fullness and a need for believers to understand the Romans 7 type conflict between good and evil that exists within us. There is no doubt that God placed the hunger deep within our souls and created a desire for us to truly know Him. The Psalmist expressed this yearning in Psalm 42: "As the deer pants for the water brooks, so my soul pants for You, O God. My soul thirsts for God, for the living God." There is a dissatisfaction, and rightfully so, with the "business as usual Christianity" that is void of the supernatural. There really is more to the Christian life than just routinely going to church. Christianity is an exciting and even thrilling experience with Jesus Christ. The closer we walk with Him, the more we realize there are spiritual conflicts existing in our world. God helps us to see where He is working and what He is doing. Jesus said in John 5:17, "My Father is working until now, and I, Myself, am working." Jesus provided us a model to follow whereby He watched to see where the Father was working and then joined in the work. Consider the words of John 5:19: "Truly, truly, I say to you, the Son can do nothing of Himself, unless *it is* something He sees the Father doing; for whatever the Father does, these things the Son also does in like manner." His work often leads to engagement of spiritual forces on multiple levels that may give us a taste of the unknown, spiritual realm where the battle for the souls of humanity is taking place in ways we cannot begin to imagine.

Potential Pitfalls

With all of that said, there are some dangers one may encounter during a study on spiritual warfare. We must be aware of these dangers and not allow them to slip into our discussion. These thoughts come from personal experience, and with some thought, you may add additional ideas to the list.

First, spiritual warfare can become romanticized in our minds; therefore, we view it unrealistically. In doing so, we become disillusioned with its reality. Battle and conflict have often been painted in unrealistic ways, thereby dulling our senses to its true horror. Consider the events around some of the opening battles of the Civil War. At the Battle of Bull Run, as forces from the North and the South began to converge on these open fields split by a stream west of Washington D.C., the good citizens of the capital city came out to enjoy the conflict as if they were attending a baseball game. Picnics were packed and finery adorned as the upper echelon of society went out to cheer on their boys. Their romanticism was dashed when they saw bodies being ripped apart and blood flowing over the fields as nearly 5,000 men were either wounded or died. Many of the spectators had to flee for their lives as the Union Army was pushed back by the Confederates. As spiritual warfare is described by those we may consider to be the spiritual elite, we have a tendency to see it all in an unrealistic way. Our focus may be on a creature slithering out of the ocean to confront a group of high school students and not on the gentle and almost imperceptible nudge to go to a pornographic website or lie to one's employer. There really is nothing glamorous about engaging the enemy of our souls who roams the earth seeking someone to devour.

A second danger is magnifying Satan through our potential obsession with spiritual warfare, turning him into more than he really is. We begin to see Satan behind every bush and give him credit for every twist and turn of life. I have heard Satan blamed for all manner of things including children's tantrums, financial troubles, and even ingrown toenails. Could tantrums not be a parenting issue, financial troubles a mismanagement of money, and toenail problems poor hygiene? When we give the devil credit, he actually receives glory. Satan really is quite limited, and we have a tendency to give him powers and abilities that he does not have. We turn him into an equal with God, but he is not! Make no mistake. Satan is powerful and formidable, but he pales in comparison to the immeasurable power of the King of Glory: the Lord Jesus Christ!

When I was five years old, I had a creature that lived under my bed, or so I thought. It all started with a dream I had in which a creature pulled someone off my bed into a stream of water that ran between the wall and my bed. The body of this poor soul went into the water, somehow disappearing, as if it had been eaten up by a monster. I could have solved my dilemma and overcome my fear if I would have just looked between the wall and my bed during the day and noted there was no stream of water, but I could not bring myself to look. As the days went on, this creature of my nightmares grew in size. It started out resembling something like Barney, but after a week or so of facing the night dreads, it turned into something that looked like a mix between an alligator, a dragon, and a one-eyed space creature with fangs. In the same way, if we are not careful, we boost Satan into a force that is stronger than God, making the church quiver in hopelessness before him.

Another danger from an improper focus and obsession on spiritual warfare is that we get caught up in the spiritual warfare mania where truth is determined by experience instead of by the Word of God. This conclusion is a huge theological catastrophe that opens the door up for all kind of heresy, and we must recognize it immediately as the demonic ploy it really is. If truth is determined by experience, then Satan can turn all manner of falsehood into truth by just helping someone to misinterpret an experience. We saw this result in our history during the revival movement of the early 1800s when people would fall onto their hands and knees and bark like a dog. They attributed this phenomenon to the moving of the Holy Spirit. While dogs do bark – annoyingly so – there is nothing in the Bible that tells us the Holy Spirit will move in this way. I am not saying that God will never do something new, but I find great security in developing my theology about the Holy Spirit and His filling from the pages of Scripture and not from an ecstatic experience. If barking in the Spirit happened in a church today, Christian pilgrims would travel to that church from all over the country hoping they, too, could experience the euphoria of barking in the Spirit.

At the risk of seeming skeptical, I believe God would have us interpret experience by truth and not interpret truth by experience. Consider the story found in the eighth chapter of the book of Acts. A magician named Simon astonished the people of Samaria with his abilities. Verse nine says that Simon claimed "to be someone great," and the people believed him. They experienced the amazing things he did, and for them, their experiences verified the truth before their eyes. They even said, "This man is what is called the Great Power of God"

(Acts 8:10). These Samaritans accepted their experiences as truth. Our perceptions about experiences can be so twisted that Satan can lead us to create all manner of theological positions that may even end up standing in opposition to the Word of God or leading individuals to glory in the experience instead of glorifying God.

I alluded earlier to another danger: developing an unbiblical view of Satan. Spiritual warfare does sound scary, and Satan does seem quite overwhelming, but I must remind myself often that Satan is not omnipotent (all powerful). He is also not omniscient (all knowing) or omnipresent (everywhere at the same time). Satan would love to have all these qualities, I am sure, but these belong only to God Almighty. Our theology must come from the pages of Scripture. If you want to know what Satan is like, don't go to Hollywood or to fictional writing. Go straight to the Truth of God. While Satan is strong and powerful, he is NOT God.

Another danger is that we blame Satan for everything, thereby abdicating our own responsibility for our spiritual failures. This excuse is as old as the Garden of Eden. If sin is our fault, then we are not only accountable for our actions, but we are also responsible to change our actions. It is so much more convenient to always blame Satan. By growing up in a home with multiple brothers and a sister, I learned at an early age that I could sometimes get away with things by blaming one of my siblings. We all learn how to play the blame game early on, and it becomes part of our standard operating procedure. Although it is true that Satan relishes in leading us to sin, we also choose to sin! I heard someone once say, "If I could kick the person most responsible for my problems, I wouldn't be able to sit down for a week." We are sinners both by nature (Satan) AND by choice (you or me).

One final danger of talking about spiritual warfare is that we focus entirely on the devil as our enemy, and this fixation causes us to minimize other lethal enemies. It is true that Satan is the enemy of our soul, but he's not the only enemy of our soul. The Bible actually mentions three enemies that are all formidable. It is possible to connect spiritual warfare to just demonic activity, but in doing so, we become easy prey for one of the other two enemies. We may even streamline our spiritual conflict to just Satan when it could be another source, and we, therefore, attack the challenge in the wrong way. It may not need to be emphasized, but we battle Satan differently than we battle the world. If we are going to stand firm in the last days, we must defeat our three arch enemies.

The World

When we think of the world as our enemy, we must be careful to realize we are not talking about the physical planet nor are we talking about the people who inhabit it. We are talking about the world's systems and philosophies. It is true that Satan influences the thinking of the people in our world and surely must influence their philosophies, but the Bible is clear that the world stands alone as a spiritual enemy. It may be that our world does not need help from Satan in developing systems or philosophies that lead us far away from God. For example, we sometimes attribute the theory of evolution to demonic activity in the mind of Darwin or someone else, but the fact is that Satan may not have placed that idea in Darwin's mind. He could have, but it is possible Darwin didn't need any help. 1 John 2:15-17 warns us: "Do not love the world nor the things in the world. If anyone loves the world, the love of the Father is not in him. For all that is in the world, the lust of the flesh and the lust of the eyes and the boastful pride of life, is not from the Father, but is from the world. The world is passing away, and *also* its lusts; but the one who does the will of God lives forever."

Lust is connected to those things we want now. Pride is the philosophy that says we are the determiners of our own destinies, and we are the center of the universe. Being that this pattern is adopted by so many people, the world's philosophies can become quite strong and difficult to overcome.

The Flesh

When we use the word "flesh," we are not talking about the membrane that covers our bones. While the Bible uses the term flesh to describe the outer covering of the body, the New Testament writers, especially Paul, use it also to describe the fallen nature and sinfulness of mankind. Author Bill Gillham defined this old sin nature as "a natural bent to rebel against God's authority, to view God as a party pooper, unnecessary in one's life, someone I can live quite well without, someone to whom I refuse to submit. In short, I refuse to acknowledge Him as my God. I am my god."[5] Although we can blame the philosophy of our world for some of our spiritual struggles, this second enemy comes from within. Actually, the tense of that verb in the previous sentence, "comes," will be determined by our relationship with Jesus Christ. When we trust Jesus as our Savior, our old nature dies (see Romans 6), so our flesh, it would seem, is defeated. The problem is that our old sin nature ingrains patterns into our thinking and actions, and these ingrained patterns continue to influence and invade us. It is true that when a person repents of his or her sin and trusts Jesus as Savior, he or she becomes a new creature in Christ. With that said, Bill Gillham pointed out that while we are made into a new spirit-creation, we have paths already created in our minds and lives that become avenues for the power of sin to bring destruction. "[God] placed this new man into the same old earthsuit. It has the same old brain with the same old, green highways in it. Uh, oh! That's going to cause a problem, because it's going to be through those old, green highways that the Evil One, through the power of sin, will try to control the new man and get him to dance to the old tune."[6]

In other words, even though our old nature has been put to death, this deceased nature leaves behind highways into our will that can lead to sin. I have likened it to a leaky basement I once had. I tried so hard to stop water from coming in, but I discovered that, once upon a time, an excess amount of water made a trench down to the bottom of my foundation and found a way into my house. Although I did all manner of things to stop future water flow, the trench was made, thereby making it easy for red, muddy water to cover my basement floor. In the same way, old patterns in our life create an easy entrance for sin. This reality is why God told us in Galatians 5:16-17, "So I say, walk by the Spirit, and you will not gratify the desires of the flesh. For the flesh desires what is contrary to the Spirit, and the Spirit what is contrary to the flesh. They are in conflict with each other, so that you are not to do whatever you want."

The Devil

The final enemy in Scripture is indeed Satan. There are a number of things said about this enemy, and with them we are warned to stay alert and lean on the power of the risen Christ. 1 Peter 5:8-9 says, "Be alert and of sober mind. Your enemy the devil prowls around like a roaring lion looking for someone to devour. Resist him, standing firm in the faith, because you know that the family of believers throughout the world is undergoing the same kind of sufferings." It is critical that we remember the devil was defeated at the cross, and his defeat was underscored with the empty tomb! Satan is a defeated foe, so we must not allow him to act like the victor in our lives. This is why 1 John 4:4 says, "The One who is in you is greater than the one who is in the world."

Obviously, we have significant preparation to do in order to be prepared for the spiritual warfare we must endure. This type of warfare is real and serious, and we must not brush it aside. If we are going to stand firm in the last days, and lead our children to do so as well, we must understand the full nature of our enemy and the dangers of a wrong focus. While we need to be tuned in to the concept of spiritual warfare and understand with clarity the nature of our enemy, the Bible clearly directs our focus to Jesus: "And let us run with perseverance the race marked out for us, fixing our eyes on Jesus, the Pioneer and Perfecter of faith. For the joy set before Him, He endured the cross, scorning its shame, and sat down at the right hand of the throne of God."[7]

PART II

How Has God Equipped Us to Stand Immovable?

Chapter Five

The Belt of Truth

Bible scholars have placed the book of Ephesians into a category of Paul's writings called the Prison Epistles. The obvious reason is because Paul wrote the four books in that group (Ephesians, Philippians, Colossians, and Philemon) while in prison. It is significant to note Paul's circumstances because it is possible that while he wrote the words of Ephesians 6:10-17, he was chained to a Roman soldier. I can imagine Paul sitting there in the early morning gloom looking at his captor, sitting next to him. If Paul were not chained to the guard at the time, there was one nearby who helped Paul draw the spiritual parallels through observation. While these verses can apply to any spiritual conflict a Christian may face throughout the history of the church, one can see how critical it is that they be applied to Christians preparing to stand firm in the last days. Throughout my life, I have considered the spiritual armor as being equipment for the daily challenges in my Christian life, and I even followed the advice of various studies to "put the armor on" every morning before getting out of bed. I think this advice is sound, and certainly this passage has equipped believers for centuries to face the conniving schemes of the evil one; however, I believe there is a special application of these truths to the believers who will be alive as humanity moves into what the Bible calls the "last days." If we are going to be prepared to be immovable during this difficult time, we must consider the significance of each piece in light of last days living. Paul mentions the first piece of armor in verse 14: "Stand firm then, with the belt of truth buckled around your waist."

When Paul said, "Stand firm then," he was using a word that means "stand upright." Author Rick Renner believes God was saying we are to stand with confidence. It also carries with it the idea of standing your ground and not being pushed back.[1] Paul makes this statement with conviction as if he has presented the two options, standing firm versus falling and failing, and his readers are choosing to stand. As Paul looked at the soldier's armor and created spiritual parallels, he started with a piece that would have been last to put on–the belt. The Roman soldier wore a leather belt on top of all his armor in order to hold everything in place. It also served as a utility belt to which he could attach things, like a sword. While the belt would have been the last thing a soldier would put on, Paul mentions it first. Is it possible he mentioned it first because the principle the belt symbolized was foundational to every other piece of spiritual armor?

The Challenge to the Truth

In light of another Scripture passage which explains that truth will be in short supply during the last days, it is significant that truth is mentioned first. Paul warned Timothy about this reality in 2 Timothy 4:1-5:

> I solemnly charge *you* in the presence of God and of Christ Jesus, Who is to judge the living and the dead, and by His appearing and His kingdom: preach the word; be ready in season *and* out of season; reprove, rebuke, exhort, with great patience and instruction. For the time will come when they will not endure sound doctrine; but *wanting* to have their ears tickled, they will accumulate for themselves teachers in accordance to their own desires, and will turn away their ears from the truth and will turn

aside to myths. But you, be sober in all things, endure hardship, do the work of an evangelist, fulfill your ministry.

Timothy was to teach and preach the Scripture carefully and constantly because there will come a time when people will eventually not put up with sound doctrine. One of the key signs of the Second Coming Jesus mentioned in Matthew 24 is deception. According to the Apostle Paul, who wrote under the inspiration of God, part of the deception would come from within. Self-deception is ruling in the hearts of humanity today as we see many examples of people who will not put up with sound doctrine. In other words, people do not care what the Bible says. This passage tells us that instead of listening to preachers, who speak the truth of Scripture in boldness, people will gather around those teachers who "say what their itching ears want to hear." Today a number of popular preachers avoid difficult or politically incorrect concepts the Bible may teach in order to focus on the topics that are more readily received by people. People would much rather hear teaching that says God is love rather than God is judge. People would rather hear that God's abundance and happiness is within their grasp rather than the consequence of sin is death. Most would rather not hear that God may even use the path of heartache to shape us a little more into the image of His Son.

Paul told the young pastor the discouraging news that a time was coming when people would not put up with "sound doctrine." To say something is "sound" means whole or well (as opposed to sick). Dictionary.com defines something that is sound as "free from damage, injury, or decay."[2] If we are going to walk across a deep gorge on a wooden bridge, we want to know if the bridge is sound. We want to know if it is whole or free from damage. Is it solid? Will it hold us up? In the last days, people do not want solid teaching that is true, rather they want teaching that will suit their own desires. Church attenders will find teachers who will support what they want. People who want wealth will find preachers who will tell them God will make them rich. Those who want happiness will find Peter Pan preachers who will only preach sermons that will help people find their happy place. Men and women who want immorality will find preachers who will preach that God is only love and not wrath.

Truth has been under attack from the beginning. One need only turn to the first book of the Bible to find Satan in the Garden of Eden putting truth under question as he persuaded Eve to eat of the fruit. From that day until today, Satan has continued to lead humanity to question the truth of God. In 2009, George Barna conducted a survey that should chill the spirit of every Christian. He found that only one-third of all adults (34%) believe that moral truth is absolute and unaffected by circumstances, and less than half (46%) of people who claim to be born-again believers believe truth is absolute.[3] While the term "absolute truth" has been discussed at length in various writings, some may not have a good grasp of its meaning. Absolute truth is that which is true for all people, for all times, and for all places. It is truth that is objective, universal, and constant. Consider this contrast of absolute truth and relative truth:

- Relative truth can be understood in two ways: All truth is relative to time and space (true then but not now), and all truth is relative to people (true for me but not for you).
- Absolute truth implies that whatever is true at one time and in one place is true at all times and in all places. Whatever is true for one person is true for all people.

Charles Swindoll expressed his concern about the slow change our contemporary culture has embraced regarding truth:

> Our world is not only ignorant of the basic facts of the Bible, most now are skeptical, convinced there is no such thing as absolute truth. The deception is so subtle we can be led to believe that what is wrong is right, and what is bad is, in fact, good, and, tragically, most people don't realize either until it is too late.[4]

The words of President Obama, from his book, *The Audacity of Hope,* express how this rejection of absolute truth is now normal in our society:

> It's not just absolute power that the Founders sought to prevent. Implicit in its structure, in the very idea of ordered liberty, *was a rejection of absolute truth*, the *infallibility* of any idea or ideology or theology or "ism," any tyrannical consistency that might lock future generations into a single, unalterable course, or drive both majorities and minorities into the cruelties of the Inquisition, the pogrom, the gulag, or the jihad. The Founders may have trusted in God, but true to the Enlightenment spirit, they also trusted in the minds and senses that God had given them. *They were suspicious of abstraction* and liked asking questions, which is why at every turn in our early history theory yielded to fact and necessity" (italics added).[5]

Are these statements by our current president true? What about the Preamble of the Declaration of Independence? "We hold these truths to be self-evident: that all men are created equal; that they are endowed by their Creator with certain unalienable rights: that among these are life, liberty, and the pursuit of happiness."

One quote that some of our liberal, historical revisionists would like to make sure never finds its way into our school text books comes from George Washington, in his first inaugural address delivered on April 30, 1789: "The propitious smiles of Heaven can never be expected on a nation that disregards the eternal rules of order and right, which Heaven itself has ordained."[6] Alexander Hamilton wrote, "In disquisitions of every kind there are certain primary truths, or first principles, upon which all subsequent reasoning must depend."[7] President Obama must have overlooked these quotes, and many others, which reveal our Founding Fathers were, for the most part, godly men who held to a strong belief in absolute truth. Sadly, this foundation is being eroded.

I think one could easily see why the enemy of our souls wants truth to be accepted as relative instead of absolute. Relative truth excuses atrocities and will ultimately make moral chaos more acceptable. Relative truth will lead humanity to accept immoral lifestyles as normal and cause people to wonder why the extreme view of religious fundamentalists is even being tolerated in our modern society. Truth is a threat to hell and must, therefore, be a goal of every believer. The only way to defend ourselves from the onslaught of moral relativity and the consequences of such a philosophy is to immerse ourselves into the solid, unalterable truth of God.

The Truth of God's Son

When Paul spoke of putting on the belt of truth, there were at least two concepts of which he spoke. The first is related to knowing God's truth. While on most occasions we immediately connect the concept of God's truth to God's Word, the first consideration must be God's Son. Consider the words of John 14:6: "Jesus answered, 'I am the way and the truth and the life. No one comes to the Father except through Me.'" Putting on the belt of truth first and foremost begins with putting on Jesus Christ. It is significant that Paul begins this whole process by calling us into a personal relationship with Jesus Christ. Before truth is a concept, truth is a Person. One cannot face the challenges of a failing economy, an unstable world, persecution, natural disasters, growing immorality, leadership failure, loss of national sovereignty, and the greatest spiritual conflict the world has known since the cross without a meaningful relationship with the Savior of our souls.

We are not strong enough on our own to endure the challenges and difficulties our world will continue to experience, nor wise enough to understand the times and be aware of the significance of world events. We are not good enough to earn God's favor and, thereby, escape the consequences of our sin. We need Jesus. The problem we have when it comes to our own goodness is that we often times allow other people to become our standard instead of Jesus Christ. It is only the righteousness of Christ that shows us our need for a Savior. Satan loves to promote a works-based salvation because he knows the truth of Romans 3:10: "There is no one righteous, not even one." If Satan can get us to believe that we can somehow be good enough to earn our salvation, then he knows we will be forever his. We need Jesus. He is the only way to salvation. Jesus will rapture His church (1 Thessalonians 4:16-18), and the only way we will be caught up to meet the Lord in the air is through a personal relationship with Jesus Christ.

Before proceeding further in exploring the spiritual armor and preparing ourselves for last days living, I must ask you if you have personally turned from your sin and surrendered your life to Jesus Christ. Have you trusted Christ's death on the cross to be the payment for your sin? Have you responded to God's call on your life to be a follower of Christ? If we are indeed moving toward the last days (or find ourselves already living in them), it is essential that you know beyond a shadow of a doubt you belong to Jesus. If you would like to read further about what this means and how to become a Christian, I encourage you to turn to the appendix which explains how to become a Christian.

The Truth of God's Word

Knowing God's truth also includes having a clear understanding of the truth of God's Word. To combat great deception during the last days, we must know the Word of God. Such understanding requires more than just a working knowledge of the basic Bible stories. It is unfortunate that we find ourselves in a time when most Americans do not even know the basic Bible stories. Sadly, for the first time in the history of our country, many Americans have no memory of biblical truths or religious experiences in their lives. While many of us cut our teeth on Bible stories, such as Zacchaeus or David and Goliath, there are many people living in our neighborhoods who would think Zacchaeus was a Greek god and David and Goliath was a punk rock band from the 80s.

I stress our need to know more than just children's Bible stories. We need to be able to engage the philosophies and beliefs of our day with the truth of the Bible and, thereby, develop a solid, biblical worldview. We now live in a world that may allow one to personally value the Bible, but that value is not welcomed in many public arenas. It is interesting how some will scorn a football player for kneeling in the end zone for a brief prayer of thanks and applaud a basketball player who publically comes "out of the closet" to announce his homosexual lifestyle. The secular mind will allow people to lean on the crutch of Christianity as long as they keep their religious perspectives to themselves, yet a blatant display of an immoral lifestyle draws a congratulatory phone call from our President.

Christians must be prepared to graciously engage people in our culture with truth from Scripture and help them see the fallacy of faulty thinking. Author Nancy Pearcey told a story of a high school teacher who divided the black board into two sections. On one section, he drew a heart and on the other a brain. He proceeded to tell the class the heart is what we use for religion, and the head is what we use for science. Pearcey said, "If all we give them is a 'heart' religion, it will not be strong enough to counter the lure of attractive, but dangerous, ideas. Young believers also need a 'brain' religion...Training young people to develop a Christian mind is no longer an option; it is part of their necessary survival equipment."[8] This challenge means we must grapple with some of the deeper thoughts of Scripture while comparing them to the liberal philosophies of our day, and we must not be content with only the spiritual baby food of the basic thoughts of the Bible. God does address many of the complex issues of our time, and we must be prepared to counter the lies of our culture with the truth of God's Word.

This kind of Bible knowledge does not come from a casual reading of Scripture. We must endeavor to become real students of the Word of God. Second Timothy 2:15 admonishes us to do so: "Do your best to present yourself to God as one approved, a workman who does not need to be ashamed and who correctly handles the Word of truth." Many of our young people are led astray by a liberal professor or an immoral friend because they are not taught to think biblically about their world and their lives. Ephesians 4:14 says, "Then we will no longer be infants, tossed back and forth by the waves, and blown here and there by every wind of teaching and by the cunning and craftiness of people in their deceitful scheming." If we are going to be prepared to deal with the lies and hypocrisy of our day, we must recognize error when we hear it. If we do not, we will be blown around by every wind, and chaos will guide the thinking and decisions of the next generation.

Understanding Your Identity

Another key to putting on the belt of truth is for believers to be true to who they are. As being a Christian becomes less and less admirable, we will find Christians beginning to waver in their commitment. Paul and Barnabus were concerned about this tendency as they thought about the churches established on the first missionary journey. Acts 14:21-22 says, "Then they returned to Lystra, Iconium, and Antioch, strengthening the disciples and encouraging them to remain true to the faith." I think the same admonition needs to be offered to Christians today. In this controversial world where truth seems to be determined by the Supreme Court or peer influence, we must be reminded that God is the source of truth. We must remain true to God and His Word. This conviction means that our actions must be in agreement with our confession. My mother used to always tell me, "Be who you are. If you're not you, who is going to be you?" I think these words of advice are a great thought for us to consider. If we're not going to wear the name of Christ publically, who will? Being a Christian in the last days means that I will be true to my confession. I will stay the course regardless of the turbulence in our society. I will trust God regardless of what goes on in the world around me.

While the first concept points to knowing God's truth, the second is maintaining an attitude of truthfulness. Because lies and deceptions will be so commonplace during the last days, truthfulness will be in short supply. Christians will present a compelling witness to the world as they show themselves to be trustworthy in all they do and say. Although we do not know exactly when Christ will return for His church, I'm going to consider the days, months, or even the last few years leading up to His return as either the last days or a precursor to the last days. It is essential that our witness be strong, for time is running out for the salvation of souls. Honesty builds trust and provides fertile ground for the gospel to take root in the lives of people within our sphere of influence. Putting on the belt of truth must call us to reflect truth in all we do.

An attitude of truthfulness means we will not only be honest in our dealings with people, but also "speak the truth in love" (Ephesians 4:15). Sometimes, we are hesitant to speak truth about life's matters, but time is running out. People need to be confronted in loving and compelling ways about the choices they are making. We must help other believers make wise choices and walk in obedience to Christ's commands, and we must point non-believers to the only One who can save them from their sins – Jesus Christ. This ministry requires speaking truth, even if it is uncomfortable to do so. Scripture admonishes us to speak the truth in love. Our motivation for truth is always love for our Savior and love for the world.

Responding to the Truth

With these concepts in mind, we are called to receive the Word of God as the standard of truth. People will always claim to know the truth or to have special inside knowledge of the truth, but the standard for truth must always be the Word of God. The Bible consistently claims to be truth. Jesus prayed in John 17:17, "Sanctify them by the truth; Your Word is truth." The Psalmist reflected upon God's truth in Psalm 25:5: "Guide me in Your truth and teach me, for You are God, my Savior, and my hope is in You all day long." Receiving God's Word means we must develop a regular plan for Bible intake, which means more than just a casual reading. We must study, memorize, and meditate upon the Scripture. In order to embrace this challenge, we must develop the discipline of carefully studying the Bible.

Another thing we must do as we move toward the culmination of time is proclaim the Word of God as the herald of truth. How do we combat those who are ear itchers (2 Timothy 4:2-3)? Someone must recognize heresy in the last days for what it is. Not only must we recognize it, but we must expose it. We must speak the truth of God with boldness as the world around us tries to hide it. The bottom line is you can never go wrong with the Word of God. It is not only the best way; it is also the only way. Don't be afraid to tell people their only hope for forgiveness and eternal life is Jesus Christ. We encounter people who say there are many ways to God, but the Bible says there is only one way to God and that is through Jesus Christ. Whenever Timothy was told to preach the Word in 2 Timothy 4:2, the term meant to proclaim with authority. Whenever we share God's Word with our friends, we are speaking under the authority of God Almighty.

Not only must we speak God's truth with boldness, but also we must speak with grace. Whenever God commands us to preach the Word, the obvious intent is for the world to hear His truth. Have you ever heard the Word of God spoken without grace? Have you ever seen the Word of God lived without grace? What do I mean about speaking the truth with grace? Colossians 4:4-6 states, "Pray that I may proclaim it clearly, as I should. Be wise in the way you act toward outsiders; make the most of every opportunity. Let your conversation be always full of grace, seasoned with salt, so that you may know how to answer everyone." When Jesus preached harshly to a crowd of people, it was always to those who were religious hypocrites. I am not saying that there is not a time to speak plain, blunt truth to someone who does not know the Lord, but that conversation that is seasoned with salt and full of grace will be something that creates thirst and feels more like a soothing ointment on a broken body.

I once stood listening to a street preacher as she told everyone they were going to hell, and she seemed to gain satisfaction from making this declaration. I've seen people look down their religious noses at mere passersby while holding signs condemning them to hell for all manner of shortcomings. I have a hard time picturing Jesus standing on the street telling the world they are going to hell. I can see Him warning them of hell while urging them to repentance and faith in Christ. While the world needs to know that eternity in hell is a reality for those who don't know Christ, they need to see and experience the love and grace of God in our lives as we lead them to personal faith in Christ in the context of a loving relationship. We all need to learn how to speak and react with grace. Do you ever just want to walk around signing people up for grace lessons? At times, I would probably need to sit on the front row of the class.

Proclaiming the Word as a herald of truth is important, but if we do not live the Word as the expression of truth, our proclamation will go unheard. Let's return to Paul's inspired words to a young pastor in 2 Timothy 4:2. Timothy was told to "correct, rebuke, and encourage with great patience and careful instruction." The context indicates God's Word is not something to just be heard and ignored. "Correct" means "to expose." It's not only to show where we are wrong but also to alter our actions. The idea is that we must use God's Word to expose faulty living, and we are to adjust our lives to God's teaching. In other words, when the Bible shows us we are doing something wrong, we change. Receiving the Word means nothing if we do not live the Word. Consider the words of James 1:22-25:

> But prove yourselves doers of the word, and not merely hearers who delude themselves. For if anyone is a hearer of the word and not a doer, he is like a man who looks at his natural face in a mirror; for once he has looked at himself and gone away, he has immediately forgotten what kind of person he was. But one who looks intently at the perfect law, the law of liberty, and abides by it, not having become a forgetful hearer but an effectual doer, this man will be blessed in what he does.

What the world so desperately needs to see in these times are Christians who live the Word of God. You can hurt the gospel message with actions that are not Christlike. Is it any wonder that some people in our culture are turned off to the Bible? If we are going to be effective in sharing our faith and in recognizing and countering deception, we must not only *know* the truth, but we must also *live* the truth. One cannot put on the belt of truth without a daily commitment to live out the truths of God.

David Jeremiah wrote about Scripture being living and active. He quoted Beth Moore as saying, "We might say that every breath comes to us still warm from the mouth of God, as if He just said it." Jeremiah added additional commentary:

> When you open this Book, you are not just opening a book. When you read the Word, you are doing more than reading words. You are not simply taking in information; you are taking in life, warm from the breath of God. Nor are you studying the works of dead writers–rather you are hearing the voice of the living Lord. And when this world is in crisis, and up seems down, and right has gone wrong, this Book holds the answers you need. You and I should inhabit its pages more fully than we reside in our physical houses. We should consume its truth as surely as we eat the food upon our tables. When there's no other visible source of confidence, we can stay confident in the Word of God.[9]

First Things First

The belt of truth is mentioned first for a reason. Without truth, every other weapon could become dulled by the relentless assaults of our spiritual enemy. It is critical that every believer make a commitment within his or her heart to know the truth and put it to practice in his or her life. When we stand tall upon the truth of God's Word, we will find that we stand above our enemies, and we will discover a renewed strength and effectiveness in the spiritual conflict as God, Who is Truth, leads us into battle.

CHAPTER SIX

The Breastplate of Righteousness

When we read relevant Scripture describing the last days, one reoccurring thought is that things will continually get worse until the Second Coming of Jesus Christ at the end of the Tribulation Period. We can only imagine the mayhem that will ensue as the seals are opened and the bowls poured out, as the book of Revelation describes. The Bible prophecies calamity that is difficult for us to picture, but it will certainly be a global crisis unlike anything the world has ever known. While there is disagreement among Bible students as to when the rapture of the church will take place, many students believe it will happen either before the Tribulation or somewhere around the halfway point of the final seven years. This timing would mean that Christians will not see the greatest upheaval to hit the world during this final period of unparalleled catastrophe. Regardless of when the rapture happens, a steady decline morally, economically, and spiritually will take place as the stage is set for final showdown between good and evil. The man the Bible calls the "Antichrist" is someone who will become a dominant world leader directing the world further and further from truth. He will eventually be totally possessed by Satan, in order to do Satan's work during the last half of the Tribulation before the final battle that will take place in a valley called Armageddon (Revelation 16:16).

Setting the Stage for the Antichrist

Though I do not believe Christians will see all the wrath of God described in the book of Revelations, I do believe we will experience the continual decline leading to fulfillment of many of the last days' prophecies that must take place before the end of the Tribulation Period and the Second Coming of Christ. According to Daniel's prophecy, the world will move into a one-world, global government during the last days (see Daniel 2:31-45). A global government will necessitate a global currency. Can you imagine all the people of the world agreeing to come together under one world leader? Can you imagine all the financial markets and global, financial leaders agreeing to burn their old currency in order to exchange it for global tender? I can imagine these changes only as I begin to study the Bible prophecies relating to global calamities. It seems the only way our country would yield to losing our national sovereignty is through a series of events that lead us to have no choice but to turn over the keys of our nation to one who seems to have answers to our national and global dilemma. You need not look far to discover the current global mess in financial markets that could easily lead to a world-wide economic collapse. It would be easy to imagine a terrorist attack or a natural disaster that would cripple our country in such a way that we have no choice but to lean upon a new, global leader for our survival.

Not only do I believe our nation, and world for that matter, will see such physical calamities as to require a global deliverer, who will ultimately be the Antichrist, but also I believe the moral/spiritual stage must be set so as to receive a leader who promotes immorality and disdains the Judeo-Christian values upon which our nation was built. Again, while it is shocking in one respect, it is easy for us to see the spiritual slide that will make national immorality an accepted practice. A few years ago, I never would have believed homosexual marriage would be accepted in the United States, but now it seems to not only be accepted, but applauded. A few years ago, I would not have imagined drugs being legalized in our country, but now, I can easily see how the rest of our country could follow Colorado's lead in legalizing marijuana. Could this be a small step that ultimately leads to open drug use of all kinds? While the sanctity of human life is disregarded, so is the sanctity of the marriage bed. I was shocked some time ago to read of websites designed to assist men and women in having extra-marital relationships, and we should all be horrified and ashamed to know it is estimated that in 2012 somewhere between $8 billion and $13 billion was spent in the United States on pornography.[1] These profits are comparable to money made by the National Football League ($9.5 billion) or Major League Baseball ($7.7 billion).[2]

Contesting the "New Normal"

Immorality is growing in America as sins that were one time committed in secret are now openly accepted. This culture of immorality will be an essential element to the world domination of the Antichrist. Considering the new normal, the second piece of spiritual armor that is needed to stand firm in the days leading up to the rapture of the church is the breastplate of righteousness. Consider again the words of Ephesians 6:14: "Stand firm then, with the belt of truth buckled around your waist, with the breastplate of righteousness in place." While considering the national slide into immorality and the disdain with which people treat the truths of Scripture, unrighteousness will be the new normal in a world heading toward Armageddon. God says if we are going to stand in the evil day, we must put on righteousness. It will be for us like a breastplate protecting the most vital organs maintaining spiritual vibrancy. Without a metal breastplate protecting a soldier's heart, he would have little hope of surviving ancient warfare. God says it is righteousness which protects this center of life for us.

Gaining a Right Standing Before God

Whenever God tells us to put on the breastplate of righteousness, there are really two concepts we must consider. Theologians think of it as "imputed" righteousness and "imparted" righteousness. While these terms may not be commonplace in our conversations, the presence of them must be commonplace in our lives. Paul presented the idea of imputed righteousness in Romans 4:1-5:

> What then shall we say that Abraham, our forefather according to the flesh, has found? For if Abraham was justified by works, he has something to boast about, but not before God. For what does the Scripture say? "ABRAHAM BELIEVED GOD, AND IT WAS CREDITED TO HIM AS RIGHTEOUSNESS." Now to the one who works, his wage is not credited as a favor, but as what is due. But to the one who does not work, but believes in Him who justifies the ungodly, his faith is credited as righteousness.

A key word for our consideration in this passage is the word "credited." Imputed righteousness is the righteousness *God puts on us* in response to His grace. This concept is critical for us to understand as we consider our standing before God. Our salvation had nothing to do with our works. Titus 3:5-7 clearly tells us our salvation was because of God's cleansing work and not because of meritorious deeds:

> He saved us, not on the basis of deeds which we have done in righteousness, but according to His mercy, by the washing of regeneration and renewing by the Holy Spirit, whom He poured out upon us richly through Jesus Christ our Savior, so that being justified by His grace we would be made heirs according to the hope of eternal life.

Imputed righteousness, then, is simply the right standing God chooses to give us thereby making us right, clean, and forgiven in His sight.

Even as receiving salvation is not dependent upon our works, keeping our salvation is also not dependent upon our works. While we could discuss all the theological foundations for this truth, my point is to emphasize that our righteous standing before God has nothing to do with our efforts. We are righteous because He makes us righteous and chooses to view us as forgiven. Much of our spiritual victory will hinge upon how we overcome the accusations of the evil one who is called the "accuser of the brothers" in Revelation 12:10. Satan's goal is first to keep people from being saved. If that cannot be accomplished and a person becomes a Christian, Satan's next objective is to keep Christians from being effective. One way to do that is to cause us to fail spiritually and to wallow around in our failure. If we can be led to think our righteousness is dependent upon our ability to do right things and that our righteousness is reliant upon our ability to be spiritually strong, then our spiritual failure is almost guaranteed.

I can imagine Satan trembling at the thought of Christians understanding the teaching of imputed righteousness. If you are a Christian, then you became righteous the moment you surrendered your life to Jesus Christ and submitted to His Lordship. The righteousness was not earned but rather credited. Let me illustrate. Suppose, out of the goodness of my heart, I go to your bank and deposit $1,000 into your account. You did not earn it, and let's say for the sake of illustrations, you do not deserve it. Your account was credited because I am a generous guy with deep pockets (remember this is an illustration). In reality, my pockets are quite shallow, but God's pockets are extremely deep. God said it this way in Ephesians 2:4-5, "But God, being rich in mercy, because of His great love with which He loved us, even when we were dead in our transgressions, made us alive together with Christ (by grace you have been saved)."

God is rich in mercy! Because He is so rich in mercy, He credited righteousness to your account the moment you became a Christian, and your account is not depleted when you make a withdrawal of His mercy. It may seem that while we start the Christian life with a large reserve of mercy, that reserve would be diminished every time we committed a sin, but this opinion is not what the Bible teaches. The moment you became a Christian, the blood of Jesus was applied to your life – your whole life – and you became a saint of God. The word "saint" in the Greek language means "holy one." You became a holy one because God set you apart for His purposes. You and I are righteous because when God looks at us, He sees us through the blood of Christ. Christ's blood makes us instantly and eternally clean. If you put on sunglasses with a red tint, everything looks red. It is almost as if God has on blood-colored glasses every time He looks at Christians, and all He sees is the blood of Jesus.

With this said, we must be quickly reminded that imputed righteousness does not give us free license to sin. Paul addressed this truth in Romans 6:1-2: "What shall we say then? Are we to continue in sin so that grace may increase? May it never be! How shall we who died to sin still live in it?" Actually, the Bible is full of instructions and admonitions to be obedient to God's commands. We have all experienced failure in our spiritual battles when we cave in and sin; therefore, we must understand the second concept connected to our righteousness: imparted righteousness. As badly as we want to live the Christian life, there is only one person who can live the Christian life – Jesus Christ. We must be like Paul and say, "I have been crucified with Christ and I no longer live, but Christ lives in me. The life I live in the body, I live by faith in the Son of God, who loved me and gave Himself for me" (Galatians 2:20).

We must also seek to understand the meaning of imparted righteousness. We can live the Christian life only by dying to ourselves and allowing Jesus to impart His righteousness through our lives. Jesus lives the Christian life through the surrendered life of His followers. Paul expressed this well through the inspiration of the Holy Spirit in Philippians 2:12-13 "So then, my beloved, just as you have always obeyed, not as in my presence only, but now much more in my absence, work out your salvation with fear and trembling; for it is God who is at work in you, both to will and to work for *His* good pleasure." Both the admonition to choose to obey and the means for obedience are expressed in these verses. While we must make daily choices to "work out" our salvation by being obedient to God's commands, we must remember that "it is God who works" in us to will and to act in a way that pleases God and fulfills our purpose to bring glory to the name of our Savior.

As our world becomes increasingly sinful, we must consider the critical role of spiritual warfare in the days leading up to the rapture of the church. People are gradually becoming desensitized to sin and immorality. For example, I am writing this chapter the day after Nik Wallenda made his now historic tight-rope (metal cable) walk across the Grand Canyon. My family and I watched in amazement at his daring and skill. We felt a sense of gratitude for the fact the whole 22 minutes it took him to cross, he was constantly giving praise to Jesus Christ and praying for God's protection. Of course, if I were walking across the Grand Canyon on a little cable, I would be praying, too. He was wearing a microphone so every word he spoke was probably heard around the world.

Our spiritual experience was interrupted with a commercial break advertising a new reality show. We sat horrified as a new survival show was advertised where men and women would be dropped naked somewhere in the world, and they would have to make it back to civilization. The thought is shocking enough, but in the advertisement during prime time, the nudity in the commercial was open and blatant. We were stunned, to say the least. Such blatant disregard for human decency would not have happened a few years ago, but somehow in our culture of lasciviousness and freedom of expression, it is now deemed acceptable. In this demonic scheme of the desensitization of America, it would be easy for Christians to be anesthetized to sin as well and fall into immoral lifestyles. We must fight against this hypnosis by wearing the belt of truth, that is knowing what is right and wrong, and by living daily in the righteousness of Christ.

Another important application of this piece of armor comes as we realize the danger of Satan's lies that can make us feel like spiritual failures. One method our enemy uses to cause us to be silent at a time when Christians should be speaking out is to make us feel unworthy to voice our opposition to the sin going on around us. He makes us feel this way by causing us to focus on our spiritual failures. How can we speak out against immorality if we have had a moral slip somewhere in our past? The way we can is to remind ourselves that while we sinned against God, His grace is sufficient enough to cleanse us and help us to move forward as cleaned, forgiven, and loved children of God. We must remind ourselves, and remind Satan, that we stand righteously before Almighty God because our moral account has been credited with righteousness. With this wonderful truth in mind, not only can we speak out against sin, but also we can share our faith with those who do not know Christ. Because we stand in the righteousness of Christ, Satan's accusations can be ignored as we tell our friends about the hope and grace we have found in Jesus Christ.

With these thoughts in mind, what must we do? We cannot just study the theological truths related to imputed and imparted righteousness, but we must act upon these truths. While I've mentioned some application points, one may wonder how to put these truths into action. There are at least two steps we must take to put on the breastplate of righteousness.

Receiving the Righteousness of Christ

The importance of making a mental and spiritual choice to receive the righteousness of Christ is emphasized in Romans 5:17: "For if, by the trespass of the one man death reigned through that one man, how much more will those who receive God's abundant provision of grace and of the gift of righteousness reign in life through the one man, Jesus Christ!" This passage points to the fact that sin was passed down to all of humanity because of Adam's sin in the Garden of Eden (Genesis 3). It says that even as sin was passed down through Adam, righteousness is made available through another man, actually a "God/man," Jesus Christ. I love the phrase "God's abundant provision of grace." God's grace is not limited! The Bible communicates that no matter how bad you are or how far away from God you are, His pockets are deep enough to contain all the grace you need.

For us to receive this righteousness, we must come to terms with our spiritual bankruptcy before God. Basically, bankruptcy is the status of a person or company that cannot repay its debts. In 2005, one out of every 55 households filed for bankruptcy in America. Thankfully, in 2012, there were about 900,000 less.[3] While that seems like a high number of bankruptcies, the Bible indicates to us that 100 percent of Americans (and for that matter, the whole world) are spiritually bankrupt. This means we all have a spiritual debt we cannot pay. Romans 6:23 reveals the payment for our sin that is required: "For the wages of sin is death, but the gift of God is eternal life in Christ Jesus our Lord." It is amazing how many people who are spiritually bankrupt still think they can somehow make restitution for their sinfulness before a Righteous Judge Who has declared them to be spiritually and morally broke. It is like they are writing checks on an account that is closed because of insufficient funds. If we are going to put on the righteousness of Christ, we must come to terms with the fact that our righteousness is actually not righteous at all!

Because God is rich in mercy, we need not roll around in our spiritual poverty nursing our depression over being destitute. To receive God's imputed righteousness, we must by faith receive our forgiveness in Christ. I love the truth expressed in 2 Corinthians 8:9: "For you know the grace of our Lord Jesus Christ, that though He was rich, yet for your sake He became poor, so that you, through His poverty, might become rich." Christ became poor so we could become rich; He died so we could have life. If you are not a Christian, it is critical for you to know that Jesus died for you so your sins could be forgiven. If you want to become a follower of Jesus, turn from your sin and receive God's forgiveness through Jesus. Satan will try to get you to think there is more to it, but based upon the authority of Scripture, your salvation is based solely upon Christ's finished work on the cross and your acceptance of God's offer of grace by surrendering your life to Him.

I do not want to minimize what it means to become a Christian. When you become a Christian, you are giving your life over to your Creator. You are not just praying a prayer, being dunked in water, or attending church services. You are becoming a follower of Jesus

Christ. You are signing the title of ownership of your life over to Jesus Christ and placing a sign in your front window that reads "Under New Management."

Once you have become a Christian, Satan will still try to make you feel unworthy and in need of forgiveness. It is because of this that I said we must "by faith, receive our forgiveness." Receiving our forgiveness will be a lifelong process, for Satan will constantly make us feel unworthy. We must remind ourselves often that the sin Satan is saying is unpardonable has already been paid for at the cross. Do you believe this truth? 1 John 1:9 says, "If we confess our sins, He is faithful and just and will forgive us our sins and purify us from all unrighteousness." All means *all*! Any sin you have committed will fall under the definition of "all." Satan wants you to feel and act unforgiven, but you must, by faith, receive the forgiveness that is yours because of the cross. When you go before God to confess your sin, you are not begging Him to forgive you. His blood was shed on the cross for all your sin. You are confessing your failure to Him and acknowledging your need, once again, for the cross. You are going before God repentant, yes, but also thankful for the cross. You and I must daily add God's grace to our account. Please understand if you are a Christian, God's grace is already there, but if you have not mentally claimed (or added) the understanding of this presence of grace to your life, you may go on living as if you are a "no-good sinner" still in need of forgiveness. This misunderstanding of grace may keep you in the clutches of Satan's sin cycle where your spiritual failure and lack of understanding of God's forgiveness leads you into greater sin.

A while back, I was balancing my checkbook. (I know for some young people who use debit cards and never enter transactions into a checkbook register, this idea may sound foreign.) When I was comparing what the bank said about my account with what I had recorded in my checkbook, I had the glorious experience of discovering I forgot to enter a deposit. I had even made some adjustments in my spending thinking my paycheck had disappeared quite quickly. I actually had money in my account all along. I just forgot to credit the money to my account. You have grace in your account. Do not treat it carelessly, but do not forget to add it to your account.

One way we add grace to our account is by acknowledging our justification through Christ. The Bible says we were made just when God gave us a complete pardon at our salvation. We are no longer enemies of God, but rather we are sons and daughters of God. God reminds us in Romans 5:1-3:

> Therefore, having been justified by faith, we have peace with God through our Lord Jesus Christ, through whom also we have obtained our introduction by faith into this grace in which we stand; and we exult in hope of the glory of God. And not only this, but we also exult in our tribulations, knowing that tribulation brings about perseverance.

Whether I feel justified or not, God says I have been made just by His eternal declaration, meaning I am on the winning side. I do not walk around in these dark days of great spiritual conflict feeling like a defeated sinner but rather like a justified saint. This teaching should give me boldness to stand against the evil one and help me to say, "No," to any further attempt by Satan or his minions to get me to fall deeper into spiritual failure. I am a soldier of God Almighty, standing in His power and because of His grace!

Acting Upon the Righteousness of Christ

Not only must we receive the righteousness of Christ, but also we must reflect the righteousness of Christ. As we think about the imparted righteousness of Christ, I'm not talking about being good in our own power, but rather choosing obedience through God's power. Reflecting Christ's righteousness is critical in the last days as sin becomes commonplace. Jesus said in Matthew 24:12, "Because of the increase of wickedness, the love of most will grow cold." Paul warned Timothy about the spiritual darkness in our world during the last days in 2 Timothy 3:1-5:

> But realize this, that in the last days difficult times will come. For men will be lovers of self, lovers of money, boastful, arrogant, revilers, disobedient to parents, ungrateful, unholy, unloving, irreconcilable, malicious gossips, without self-control, brutal, haters of good, treacherous, reckless, conceited, lovers of pleasure rather than lovers of God, holding to a form of godliness, although they have denied its power; avoid such men as these.

While all of this evil is going on around us, it is essential that we surrender daily to the Holy Spirit and walk in the righteousness of Christ. Note that verse five says there will be people with a "form of godliness but denying its power." In other words, there will be people in the last days resembling godliness, but deep down they are disobeying God and not experiencing His power. Such deception means our communities will be filled with people who call themselves Christians, but deep down, their hearts are far from God. I recently heard of someone who had lunch with Dr. Billy Graham. This pastor asked Dr. Graham if he still agreed with something the great evangelist said years ago when he declared that he thought fifty percent of church members were not believers. Dr. Graham said he no longer believed it to be fifty percent, but much higher.[4]

As the rapture of the church draws ever closer, we must realize that our churches will be filled with people who are religious but have no relationship with Jesus. Influencers will be all around us who seem to be Christian, but in reality they are far from the Lord. The only way we will stand against Satan and his temptations, as well as maintain a strong witness before a lost world, is for us regularly to put on the breastplate of righteousness.

While standing against Satan and his scheming tactics seems to be all about defense, it can also be about offense. Romans 6:11-14 presents two important points:

> Even so consider yourselves to be dead to sin, but alive to God in Christ Jesus. Therefore do not let sin reign in your mortal body so

> that you obey its lusts, and do not go on presenting the members of your body to sin as instruments of unrighteousness; but present yourselves to God as those alive from the dead, and your members as instruments of righteousness to God. For sin shall not be master over you, for you are not under law but under grace.

Paul admonished the Roman Christians to count themselves to be dead to sin and alive to God. This concept is the same as we looked at above where we are commanded to credit righteousness to our spiritual account. Verse twelve says we are not to let sin reign in our mortal body. We must remind ourselves daily that sin is a dethroned monarch in our lives. Sin and Satan do not have a throne, or even a stool, in our lives. We must make the choice to submit to Christ and receive His imparted righteousness. When verse eleven tells us to count ourselves dead to sin, Paul used a present tense verb. In the Greek language, a present tense verb means continuous action. In other words, He is saying, "keep on counting yourselves to be dead to sin every day of your lives until Christ returns." If we are going to walk in Christ's righteousness, we must win this spiritual battle in our minds by reminding ourselves, and anyone else who is listening, that we belong to Christ.

Note the second concept in this passage is focused more on offense. While we are not to present ourselves as instruments of unrighteousness, we *are* to present ourselves as instruments of righteousness. God says you are to offer "every part of yourself" to Him. Note the contrast between the two concepts of presenting or offering. To offer means "to place beside or near, to present, to proffer, to put at one's disposal."[5] He is basically saying, "Do not place yourself at sin's disposal, but rather place yourself at God's disposal."

The first "present" in Romans 6:13 is present tense, or continuous action: "Do not go on presenting the members of your body to sin." The second time "present" is used, Paul uses a different tense; therefore, he wanted to make a different point. The tense is similar to our past tense, indicating it is a once and for all declaration. It's like

God is saying, "Christian, you have given yourself to Me and have given every member of your body to Me, so live like it." If we are going to "live like it," we must daily get dressed in the breastplate of righteousness. We must daily remind ourselves that King Jesus sits on the throne of our hearts, and because our redemption was settled at the cross thousands of years ago, we can face the evil one and do the right thing. In so doing, we win battle after battle against the tempter and hater of our souls, and we reflect the righteousness, power, and love of Jesus to a world in darkness looking for the light.

CHAPTER SEVEN

Readiness of the Gospel of Peace

I prefer to be ready for anything. Few things are worse than being caught somewhere unprepared. I can think of many times I was unprepared, like the time my brother and I were backpacking on the Appalachian Trail and found ourselves in deep snow when only rain was predicted in the forecast. At other times in my life, I simply did not have an umbrella when it began to rain, or I forgot about an important school assignment as I walked into class on the day it was due. No one wants to be unprepared. Our next piece of armor deals with the concept of being ready.

This entire book is about being ready to stand firm in the last days, but putting on this next piece of armor includes a special focus on "preparation." If you think about it, being able to stand firm requires preparation, and without this preparation, we will certainly fail. The whole idea of a challenge to stand firm indicates the converse is also true. While we can, and hopefully will, stand firm, it is also possible that we will not stand firm. If you are not standing firm in the last days, you will fall or fail. The concept of standing firm is easy for us to grasp when we consider a sporting contest, like a football game. It is critical that a defensive line of a football team stand their ground when the offensive line moves toward them at the snap of the ball. Standing firm in spiritual conflict, however, is far more significant than a sports team strategy; to fail means more than just losing a game. It could prove fatal for you and affect other people in significant, negative ways. This spiritual conflict is so critical that God warns us to "put on the full armor of God, so that you can take your stand against the devil's schemes" (Ephesians 6:11). As we consider the total impact of Ephesians 6:10-18, we must not be satisfied with just one or two pieces of spiritual armor. We must be fully dressed for battle, or we may possibly fall. While we are given instructions in Ephesians 6 on how to stand firm, verse 14 makes the words "stand firm" an imperative. As an imperative, God is not offering a mere, casual suggestion; instead, He is giving us a firm command. Jesus Christ, our commanding officer, has given us an order that must be obeyed, so we must carefully consider each of the pieces of armor that will help us stand in the evil day.

The Trustworthiness of the Bible

If you are not sure you are a Christian, it is important to know that those who are not Christians *will* fall in the evil day. While some may scoff at this concept of an "evil day," we need only to consider all other Bible prophecies. For those looking at the Scripture with a skeptical eye, they should note the Bible has never been wrong in the area of prophecy or history or any other area. It is significant that the Bible spoke of ancient civilizations, which were lost thousands of years ago and forgotten. Years ago, many people discredited the Bible because it spoke of a group of people called the "Hittites." The Old Testament refers to these people 40 times, but if you lived before 1912, you may as well have been talking about Atlantis or Brigadoon. In 1912, Hugo Winckler and Theodore Makridi Bey discovered the Hittite Legal Code that explained Abraham's choice to purchase the Cave of Machpelah from Ephron the Hittite (Genesis 23). We may wonder why he bought only a cave instead of a whole tract of land, but this discovered code showed that had Abraham bought the whole tract, he would have been required to participate in a pagan ritual.[1] He obviously did not want to participate in a pagan act of worship. While the Hittites may seem to be insignificant to us, they are quite significant in that the discovery of these people gives additional proof to the authenticity of the Bible.

It is noteworthy that almost thirty percent of the Bible is made up of prophecy.[2] If one prophecy did not come true, the whole Bible would be suspect. Significant also is that no archeological discovery has ever disproven the Bible, but rather affirmed it to be true. Think about that statement for a moment. Of all the archeological discoveries made in modern time, every one that has a Bible connection has confirmed the authenticity of the Word of God. It is as if God is providing us rock-solid evidence that the Bible is valid. For those of us who believe the Bible to be God's Word, we have no trouble accepting what it says to be true, with or without archeological discoveries or prophetic accuracies. However, for those who struggle with believing the Bible, this fact is an essential concept to be considered. It is rational and logical to conclude that if every prophecy of the Bible relating to the past has come true, then we can be confident that every prophecy relating to the future will also come true.

The Bible prophesied the "evil day" is coming, and times will be extremely difficult. If we are not ready, we will not stand, and if we do not help others get ready, they will not stand. Many people will fall during the days leading up to the rapture of the church, and many, many more will fall during the final days of the Tribulation Period. Before the church is raptured, times will become increasingly more difficult, so we must be prepared to stand.

The Importance of Traction

The next piece of armor that prepares us for readiness is found in Ephesians 6:14-15, which says, "Stand firm then, with the belt of truth buckled around your waist, with the breastplate of righteousness in place, and with your feet fitted with the readiness that comes from the gospel of peace." We have moved from our waist to our chest and down to our feet. While we are somewhat acquainted with a first century soldier's footwear, we are more familiar with that of a modern-day athlete. A baseball player wears cleats to maintain traction on the baseball field. Have you ever tried to play a sport while wearing slick tennis shoes? If you are wearing only tennis shoes and try to fake out the defender while running a pass play in a football game, you may end up on your face instead of in the end zone. Roman soldiers wore something that might be considered first century cleats that would give them traction in battle for both defense and offense. As we look at this important piece of spiritual equipment, we can consider it both for defensive and offensive purposes.

Regarding defense, it would have been important in the first century world for a Roman soldier to maintain traction during an onslaught of the enemy. The enemy formed a line and moved toward the Roman soldiers as one unit, very much like an offensive line of football players move against the defense at the snap of a football. It was important for the soldiers to hold their ground because a Roman battle line would only be as strong as its weakest soldier. If one soldier went down, the whole line was in danger. While defense was important, the Roman army was clearly concerned about offense as well. As Roman soldiers moved against armies in the effort of gaining additional territories, maintaining their footing was crucial to military success. I can imagine Paul sitting on the floor chained to a Roman soldier, who sat dozing against the wall of the cell taking an afternoon nap. As Paul watched him sleep, he noticed the hobnail sandals worn by this fearless warrior and thought of how important it was for Christians involved in spiritual warfare to be able to stand against the attacks of their spiritual enemies. Perhaps the first thing that came to Paul's mind when he saw the sandals was the importance of Christians being ready for whatever comes their way.

Jesus warned us with a similar message in Matthew 24:44: "So you also must be ready, because the Son of Man will come at an hour when you do not expect Him." Four words come to mind when I consider this concept of being ready: opposition, difficulty, danger, and preparation. We have already considered our opposition at length and should know that we are standing against a formidable enemy determined to bring about our destruction. People oftentimes minimize difficulty and danger, but it is paramount we realize the challenges that are soon to come. We cannot even begin to understand the difficulty and danger people will experience in the days leading up to the rapture of the church. Most of us were raised during times of plenty and have no concept of rationing food or being unable to afford gasoline. Even though fuel has continued to increase in cost, it has not hindered most Americans from travel. Most of us have lived in times of civility where neighbors took care of neighbors and rights were considered sacred. When the wheels of society begin to come off, the unexpected will become the norm, and the perilous will become commonplace. It is critical that we are prepared and ready.

Our tendency is to think of personal readiness and family preparedness, but we also have an obligation to our world. This time of societal upheaval will provide Christians with a great opportunity for evangelism and ministry. Many people will be asking questions and looking for answers. God commands believers in 1 Peter 3:15 to exist in a state of readiness for these opportunities that come our way: "But in your hearts revere Christ as Lord. Always be prepared to give an answer to everyone who asks you to give the reason for the hope that you have. But do this with gentleness and respect." Our first step of readiness is to make sure we "revere Christ as Lord," but our second step is to be prepared to help others find answers to their spiritual perplexities.

What is the Gospel of Peace?

The question we must consider is, "What is the means by which we make this preparation?" Ephesians 6:15 says the readiness comes from the "gospel of peace." It would be easy to be enamored with the illustration of the Roman soldier and forget all about the truth each piece of armor represents. God says the "gospel of peace" is essential if we are going to stand in the last days before He calls His church home. While we are quite familiar with the word "gospel," I am afraid we do not grasp the full significance of the term. On the surface, it means "good news," but below the surface, a goldmine of wealth can be unearthed. According to 1 Corinthians 15:3-4, the good news is that Jesus died on a cross for the sins of humanity. He was buried and rose again three days later, thereby proving He is indeed God wrapped in flesh.

Christ's death, however, was not just the misfortune of a man wrongly accused. He was dying on a cross to satisfy God's law and to communicate God's grace. The Bible clearly indicates the penalty for sin is death, and every human is a sinner. The cross is a means by which God offers all of humanity an option for the salvation of their souls. We must choose from one of two possibilities. The first is that we pay for our own sins through eternal death and separation from God for all of eternity in the hell that was prepared for Satan and his followers. The second option is that we surrender our lives to the lordship of Jesus Christ, allowing His payment on the cross to become payment for our sin. The gospel, which paints a vivid picture of Christ's suffering on the cross, also underscores the seriousness of our sin and the lostness of humanity.

We have a tendency to whitewash the blackness of our own hearts and make our sins look less egregious than they really are. We have various ways to minimize our sins, like giving them colors (white lies, gray areas, etc.) or new names (instead of lying, we are reckless with the truth), but the fact is, sin is sin, regardless of the color. The prophet Isaiah said that our righteousness is like a "filthy rag" (Isaiah 64:6), which is a gentle way of saying that our best efforts are a putrid stench in the nostrils of God. The "filthy rag" term the prophet used is the Hebrew word for the dirtiest cloth you can imagine, like a dirty diaper. With that thought, you can see what God thinks of our efforts to generate our own righteousness. Throughout the Scripture, God emphasizes our spiritual bankruptcy and our desperation for a Savior. Without God's incredible mercy and grace, we would be hopelessly lost!

This gospel of peace is a gentle plea to all of humanity to come to salvation through Jesus Christ. While the gospel underscores the depth of our depravity, it also emphasizes the overwhelming magnitude of God's grace. Throughout the Scripture, God offers a universal invitation to whoever will respond. Consider the words in Revelation 22:17: "The Spirit and the bride say, 'Come.' And let the one who hears say, 'Come.' And let the one who is thirsty come; let the one who wishes, take the water of life without cost."

We see in page after page of God's Word that peace is at the very heart of God. While sin is the absence of peace, grace and mercy extend an expression of peace. The word "peace" was a part of the Hebrew greeting. The term *shalom* was a familiar sound to the Jewish ear of Bible times. It is this peace that is robbed by the sinfulness of humanity, and it is this peace that is restored through salvation. Theologian Cornelius Plantinga helps us to understand the offer of *shalom* with the following words:

> The webbing together of God, humans, and all creation in justice, fulfillment, and delight is what the Hebrew prophets call *shalom.* We call it peace, but it means far more than mere peace of mind or a cease-fire between enemies. In the Bible, shalom means *universal flourishing, wholeness, and delight* – a rich state of affairs in which natural needs are satisfied and natural gifts fruitfully employed, a state of affairs that inspires joyful wonder as its Creator and Savior opens doors and welcomes the creatures in whom He delights. Shalom, in other words, is the way things ought to be.[3]

When we consider the concept of biblical peace, we could look at it from three perspectives. The first would simply be peace with God. We are born with a nature to sin, and the Bible actually calls us the enemies of God (Romans 8:7). Paul underscored the significance of the grace of God and the offer of God's peace in Colossians 1:19-20, "For it was the Father's good pleasure for all the fullness to dwell in Him, and through Him to reconcile all things to Himself, having made peace through the blood of His cross; through Him, I say, whether things on earth or things in heaven." As we prepare to stand firm in the last days leading up to the rapture of the church, we must have peace with God, which is salvation. If we do not have peace with God, we will be left behind as the church is called up to meet the Lord in the air.

Not only is peace with God critical for last days living, but also peace with ourselves is essential if we are going to stand strong against the attacks of the evil one. Inner conflict can be created by a variety of challenges, and we have all experienced them in one way or another. Inner turmoil can be caused by not accepting God's forgiveness for our sins. Satan is quite skilled at making us feel defeated and inferior. The Scripture calls him the "accuser of the brothers" (Revelation 12:10), and he has found an effective tool in whispering condemnation into our spiritual ears. If he can maintain inner spiritual conflict in our hearts, then we have a tendency to be weak on the battlefield and ineffective in spreading the truth of God's redeeming grace. Other times, we find the lack of inner peace creeping into our lives when we are at odds with a fellow believer or fall into sinful practices that we know to be wrong and contrary to our commitment to Christ. Peace comes to Christians when our actions stand in agreement with our commitment. If our actions are more of a contradiction to our confession, we are twisted and in turmoil with ourselves. One of the great results of the cross and of God's grace is inner peace. Jesus said, "Peace I leave with you; My peace, I give you. I do not give to you as the world gives. Do not let your hearts be troubled and do not be afraid" (John 14:27). Author and speaker Dr. Larry Richards, addressed this spiritual conflict in the following passage:

> While God calls us to peace, Satan calls us to chaos. Satan wants us to live in a constant state of hurt, shame and hostility. Satan wants us to respond with bitterness and anger when we are wounded. Satan wants us to live on edge, constantly on guard. Satan wants us to be in turmoil, suspicious of others' motives and quick to take offense. Satan wants us to remember and to nurse every hurt. And,

because all human beings sin, there are occasions galore for Satan to lead us into chaos.[4]

Peace with God and peace with ourselves makes it possible to be at peace with others. Sin causes us to turn in toward ourselves, but salvation enables us to embrace others. Because of the gospel of peace and because our sins are forgiven, we can forgive others. Actually, we *must* forgive others. Contained in the model prayer of the Sermon on the Mount, we see where God expects us to offer forgiveness as part of our normal expression of His grace: "And forgive us our debts, as we also have forgiven our debtors" (Matthew 6:12). Because we are forgiven, we can now forgive. The church of Jesus is a grace-filled community. God used Paul to admonish us: "If it is possible, as far as it depends on you, live at peace with everyone" (Romans 12:18). The unity of the church is a key theme of the New Testament, but with a little thought, one can see the critical nature of our unity during times of global crisis. We will need the strength we draw from one another, and the world will need the church to be unified so the message of the gospel will be clear, and the world will know that Jesus is the Messiah.[5]

Fitted Feet for the Last Days

We are told to have our feet fitted with the readiness that comes from the gospel of peace. What is the significance of this statement for living in the last days? How will this piece of armor help the church stand firm as she awaits the return of her Groom? We have established in previous chapters that the last days will be times of great turmoil. If we are not standing in readiness from the gospel of peace, we may be swallowed up in the incredible chaos that is sure to come. It will be easy for the saints of God to become anxious as times become increasingly difficult. We do not need anxiety, but rather we need peace. Paul challenged the church in Philippians 4:4-7: "Rejoice in the Lord always. I will say it again, Rejoice! Let your gentleness be evident to all. The Lord is near. Do not be anxious about anything, but in every situation, by prayer and petition, with thanksgiving, present your requests to God. And the peace of God, which transcends all understanding, will guard your hearts and your minds in Christ Jesus." The church is told to rejoice, regardless of her circumstances. Our gentleness should be evident to all as a living testimony of the grace and power of Almighty God. When we hand our struggles to the Lord through prayer, these verses tell us that God's peace will set guard over our hearts (emotions) and minds (intellect). When the church faces the challenges of the future with a display of inner peace, the power of this witness to the world will be compelling. Many people could come to trust Jesus as Savior simply through the faith of believers who place their hope in Jesus. A drowning person always reaches for that which is stable and secure. As the rapture of the church draws ever closer and the "birth pains" of Matthew 24 are growing with intensity, the hearts of unbelievers will grow ever more fertile and open to the message of the gospel. A fearful world will be drawn to hopeful believers, and we will find this period to be a time for a rich harvest for the Kingdom of God.

Christians will also need the gospel of peace because the days ahead will be times of great spiritual conflict. No doubt, the spiritual battle will grow in intensity as the return of Christ draws closer. Paul gave us a warning in 2 Thessalonians 2:1-3:

> Concerning the coming of our Lord Jesus Christ and our being gathered to him, we ask you, brothers and sisters, not to become easily unsettled or alarmed by the teaching allegedly from us – whether by a prophecy or by word of mouth or by letter – asserting that the day of the Lord has already come. Don't let anyone deceive you in any way, for that day will not come until the rebellion occurs and the man of lawlessness is revealed, the man doomed to destruction.

Remember that the "Day of the Lord" is probably a reference to the second coming of Christ, which will take place at the end of the Tribulation Period. Regardless of when you may believe the rapture will happen, we can agree upon the fact that many of the signs of

Christ's return will start gradually before the church is taken away. Though these signs will reach their zenith at the end of the Tribulation, the church will experience them at some level before she is removed from this world. This passage above indicates deceptive teaching will become commonplace by those who may have been entrusted with the truth. This was already the case in the first century when Paul originally wrote this passage. He says in this passage that Christ's second coming will not happen until "the rebellion occurs and the man of lawlessness is revealed." It is my opinion that this "rebellion" and "lawlessness" will not be sudden happenings but rather a gradual slide into immorality. This understanding means the rebellion will begin before the rapture, and the spirit of lawlessness, which will be necessary to embrace "the man of lawlessness," will be expressed. A culture of lawlessness will bring about great spiritual conflict on battlefields we may never know about, but we can be sure the conflict is severe nevertheless. The only way we can stand secure as the onslaught intensifies is if we are wearing the cleats of the gospel of peace.

I have already emphasized the deception that will take place during the last days (including the days leading up to the rapture of the church). If we are not standing confidently, fortified by the gospel of peace, we could easily fall prey to the deception. Sometimes, this deception comes from those we may perceive to be spiritual leaders. Paul even warned us about this in 1 Timothy 4:1-2: "The Spirit clearly says that in later times some will abandon the faith and follow deceiving spirits and things taught by demons. Such teachings come through hypocritical liars, whose consciences have been seared as with a hot iron." Paul characteristically does not mince words as he refers to these false teachers as hypocritical liars. We are seeing evidence of such deception all around us. One example is from Bishop John Shelby Spong, an Episcopal Bishop of Newark, New Jersey, who wrote a book entitled *Why Christianity Must Change or Die.* He said the first-century ideas that shaped the New Testament are hopelessly outdated and provincial and must be discarded if Christianity is to survive in the modern world.[6] We can be sure that in the days ahead, heresy and deception, by people who are respected as teachers of truth, will increase. Satan will use such deception with blind, immature Christians, thereby opening them up to the chaos and upheaval that is sure to come. As people are taken in by such false teaching, they will fall in the spiritual conflict, and if they are unbelievers, they will be lost for eternity. If they are believers, they will be rendered ineffective in the spiritual battle.

Satan is using such deception to divide the church and weaken the army of the Lord. Part of putting on the gospel of peace means the church must recognize this false teaching for what it is and stand united together on the truth of God's Word. We were admonished in Ephesians 4:3 to "make every effort to keep the unity of the Spirit through the bond of peace."

Unparalleled Opportunities

I've mentioned several times how open the world will become to the message of the gospel. Another reason the gospel of peace is included in our spiritual armor is that the last days will be times of great evangelistic opportunity. Jesus said in Matthew 24:14, "And this gospel of the Kingdom will be preached in the whole world as a testimony to all nations, and then the end will come." One reason the gospel will spread around the world is because of the desperation of people. In the midst of such desperation, we have the answer that brings peace that passes understanding. The Bible teaches the only way to have peace with God is through Jesus Christ. We are about to move into times of unparalleled opportunities to share our faith, and the church must be ready and willing. Unfortunately at a time of such great opportunity, the church is exhibiting great apathy. Part of this apathy comes from the church buying in to the philosophy of our contemporary society. It is an inclusive philosophy based upon relative truth that says all beliefs are equally valid and should, therefore, not be challenged. David Platt summarized the climate of our society with these words: "In this system of thinking, faith is a matter of taste, not of truth. The cardinal sin, therefore, is to claim that one person's belief is true and another person's belief is false. The honorable route is to rest quietly in what you believe and resist the urge to share your beliefs with someone else."[7]

An evangelistic fire must be lit under the church because the world is desperate for the truth we know. It is perplexing as to why Christians who believe that Jesus is the only way to the Father remain silent, thinking that somehow in the end their friends will be okay without Christ. If we really believe the Bible, then we know that Jesus Christ is coming back for His church, and those who do not know Him will be left behind. It is troubling today that most Christians never share their faith while the cults and false teachers are fervently sharing their messages. Thom Rainer said that eighty-two percent of the unchurched are at least somewhat likely to attend church if they are invited.[8] This statement means that more than eight out of ten people who do not attend church right now would possibly come to church if they were simply invited. We can assume that most of these people, if not all of them, are lost without Jesus and desperate for the gospel message they could hear and experience through attending a Bible believing/Bible teaching church. Part of putting on the shoes of readiness means we are prepared to share the gospel of peace. C. S. Lewis stated succinctly, "The church exists for nothing else but to draw men into Christ, to make them 'little Christs.' If they are not doing that, all the cathedrals, clergy, missions, sermons, even the Bible itself, are simply, a waste of time. God became Man for no other purpose."[9]

How to Put On Your Shoes

Although we have comprehensively expressed our need for the gospel of peace, the real question now is "How do you put it on?" It begins by thoroughly knowing the gospel. This knowledge must begin in our heart, as Proverbs 1:7 says, "The fear of the Lord is the beginning of knowledge." Knowing the gospel of peace requires us to know the Giver of the gospel of peace: Jesus Christ. The Proverb writer said knowledge begins with the "fear of the Lord," and this fear points to reverential awe. It involves giving God His rightful place as Sovereign and Lord. "Knowing" involves our intellect, but it must also include our experience. We must carefully study the Scripture and mine the priceless gems found in understanding the total meaning of the gospel message. Many Christians consider the gospel to be a message only for the unbeliever, but this basic truth has implications for every believer at any stage of spiritual maturity. Throughout the Bible, we learn that our knowledge of God results in good judgment as God's truths are applied to daily living.

I urge you to ponder deeply the truth of God's grace and consider seriously the implications of mankind's depravity. As we understand our sin, God's grace and mercy are magnified, and we are fortified for the spiritual battles that await us.

We also put on the gospel of peace by meditating upon the three areas of peace described above: peace with God, peace with ourselves, and peace with others. As we consider the possibilities of peace in response to the gospel, we are more likely to be able to apply its truth to every area of our lives. This application is really an act of faith as we embrace the truth of God's peace in every circumstance. While it is natural to be anxious, we will find we can live supernaturally through the gospel message and find the peace of God standing guard over our hearts and minds. This peace will affect many areas of our lives including prayer, worship, fellowship, and discipleship.

Finally, be ready to communicate effectively the gospel of peace. Peace is the one thing every human being desires, and we have the key ingredient that makes peace a reality – the gospel. Communicating the gospel involves being prepared to share your own faith story with those who do not know Christ. It would also be helpful to learn a few basic verses that would be useful in leading others to faith in Christ, such as John 3:16, Romans 3:23, Romans 5:8, Romans 10:9-10, Ephesians 2:8-9, and 1 John 1:9. Our world has anything but peace, but we have the source of peace and the One for whom the whole world longs: Jesus Christ.

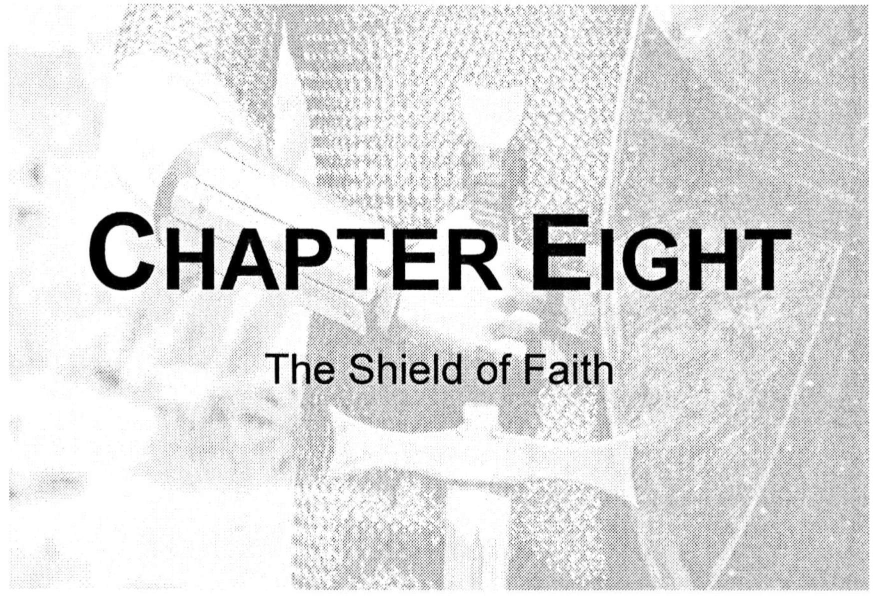

Chapter Eight

The Shield of Faith

We go to great lengths to insure our protection. Our homes are protected from burglars by security alarms, our cars are protected from thieves by alarm systems, and even our iPhones are protected with automatic locator apps. We buy insurance for our homes and cars, and some people have weapons in their homes and licenses to carry pistols in public. Protection is a big deal. We want our families to be safe, and we want our stuff to be protected.

With all this interest in protection, it is amazing to me that we may be least protected in the area that causes the greatest threat. A huge battle is being waged all around us for the souls and testimonies of people. I say "souls and testimonies" because Satan first wants our soul. If he can keep us from trusting Christ as our Savior, he has us for eternity. Once we surrender our lives to Jesus Christ, thereby acknowledging His lordship over us, Satan then works to rob us of our testimony and to make us weak in our spiritual lives. John 10:10 describes the thief who comes to rob from the shepherd, but I believe Jesus is also talking about the ultimate thief, the devil himself, when He said, "The thief comes only to steal and kill and destroy..." The thief is working hard today to steal, kill, and destroy people all around us.

While he is working his plot to defeat the King of the Ages, Almighty God also has a plan with a guaranteed conclusion. Amazingly, Satan thinks he can thwart God's intentions, but we know that God's plans will not be diverted. The Bible gives us great detail as to how events are going to progress to a certain end. As you read the prophetic portions of the Bible and consider our current events, it becomes quite clear that God is setting the stage for the final chapter of the world as we know it. Dr. David Jeremiah said, "I think any honest person must admit that something big is going on in the world. The prophecies of Daniel show us what it is: the hands on the prophetic clock are moving toward midnight. The warning has been sounded, and we will do well to heed it."[1]

Dr. Jeremiah's words, "the warning has been sounded," make me think of the alarm system in our church building going off indicating movement in a place where no one should be at the time. What would I do if I happened to be in our church building late one night and discovered an intruder was in the building with me? Without a doubt, my first move would be to call 911. My second move would probably be to run out of the building. Well, maybe I would run out of the building first and then make the call. I am a lot braver from a distance.

This chapter is about our 911 call when the thief comes to steal, kill, and destroy. Ephesians 6:16 commands us, "In addition to all, taking up the shield of faith with which you will be able to extinguish all the flaming arrows of the evil one." We could say taking up our shield of faith is the equivalent of making our 911 call. We have already looked at Ephesians 6:12 and seen how God underscores the seriousness of our battle: "For our struggle is not against flesh and blood, but against the rulers, against the powers, against the world forces of this darkness, against the spiritual forces of wickedness in the heavenly places."

Our Spiritual Struggle

Paul used a Greek athletic term when he chose the word that is translated as "struggle." One theologian defined the term as "a contest between two in which each endeavors to throw the other, and which is decided when the victor is able to press and hold down his prostrate antagonist, namely, hold him down with his hand upon his neck."[2] Kenneth Wuest stated in his renowned study on Greek words, "When we consider that the loser in a Greek wrestling contest had his eyes gouged out with resulting blindness for the rest of his days, we can form some conception of the Ephesian Greek's reaction to Paul's illustration."[3]

I mentioned in a previous chapter that the Greek word translated as *struggle* describes hand-to-hand combat with our mortal enemy. A scene comes to my mind of an American soldier huddled down in his fox hole as the First World War rises to its zenith. He hears a slight sound, and suddenly, an enemy soldier hurdles himself over the side of the hole and is on top of the American with a drawn knife. A struggle ensues in the most intense way as the two men fight face to face knowing that only one of them would crawl out of the hole alive. Our battle with Satan is serious and intense. It is a hand to hand battle where the perspiration of our enemy drips upon our face, and his hot, foul breath is inhaled by our nostrils. In that intense moment that may only be brief, war is being waged while we struggle for spiritual mastery.

God says that as our enemy approaches, we must lift up our shield of faith. It seems doubtful the soldier guarding Paul would have had a shield with him; however, Paul still connected the soldier's shield, that either leaned against the wall or was stored somewhere, to the faith that is necessary if we are going to leave a spiritual skirmish as the victor. Faith means we believe God regardless of the circumstances. It means whether we understand what's going on or we don't have a clue, we still hold on to God and know that He is somehow working His plan. I mentioned earlier that we can expect a one-world government toward the end of this age, and such unification will necessitate global failure and an economic merger. This type of change points to instability, hardship, crisis, and challenges that could overwhelm the unsuspecting person. As we move down a path that ultimately leads to the rapture of the church, we must ask ourselves if we are ready to believe God. Just the instability of our world right now could certainly lead to times of difficulty requiring great faith.

God's Control in World Events

The thirty-eighth chapter of Ezekiel speaks of a coming war between Israel and a five-nation coalition, who is in alliance with Russia. This battle is often referred to as the Battle of Gog and Magog. I believe this event in Ezekiel is different from the battle mentioned in Revelation 20:8. Though both are referred to as Gog and Magog, they seem to be pointing to two different time periods. I have wondered if the Revelation passage is pointing to a battle that will be reminiscent of Gog and Magog. This type of comparison is not uncommon in the pages of Scripture. For example, Isaiah referred to Israel as Sodom and then Gomorrah in Isaiah 1:10 as Isaiah reflected upon the sinfulness of the Jewish people. Israel was not really called "Sodom," but her sin was reminiscent of Sodom. We know that Magog referred to a region in the north that we know today as being Russia. Ezekiel lists the names of five nations that will align with Russia for this attack, and then he concludes the list by saying there will be others as well. Ezekiel used the ancient names for these places, but we can readily note that Persia is modern day Iran, Cush is the Ethiopian/Sudan region, and Put is modern day Libya. The final two nations who align with Russia are a little more difficult to determine. We do not know for certain the identity of the remaining two nations, but many theologians think Gomer is modern day Germany while Beth Togarmah is Turkey. This prophecy came to my mind recently as I listened to a news report of a brief comment by the leader of Turkey criticizing Israel. It cemented in my mind that Turkey could indeed be a part of the forthcoming coalition.

This future battle will be horrific, and Israel will stand alone against such unbelievable opposition. Ezekiel offered a prophetic hint of other nations "slapping the wrists" of Russia and her allies for engaging in such banter, which ultimately leads to war, but no one really stands against the coalition. Where are Israel's allies in this future event? Obviously, they will disappear by this time or have buried their heads in the sand. I can't help but see the early stages of this shift as the United States slowly pulls away from our long-time friends in the Middle East and seems to grow closer to various Muslim nations. Great Britain's friendship with Israel has seemed to cool, and much of the world is speaking out against the Jews. Currently, Israel and Gaza are fighting as Israel is retaliating against Hamas for firing missiles across the border. The global response to Israel defending itself against this military threat has been shocking. Instead of the world backing Israel, the consensus seems to be a unified criticism. I would be totally confused if I did not know that a global polarization against Israel was prophesied in the Bible. By the time the Battle of Gog and Magog happens, the United States will no longer have strong ties with Israel. If you read the passage in Ezekiel, you see that Israel wins the battle, or maybe I should say God wins the battle for Israel.

I can see Iran, and others, attacking Israel at some point in the future, but it seems this attack is still sometime in the future, for more provocation is needed by Israel. If you have followed the news in the past, you know great unrest currently exists with threats of war. It is difficult to forget Israeli Prime Minister Benjamin Netanyahu's "red line" illustration that he presented to the United Nations back in September of 2012 indicating the point of no return on an Iranian nuclear attack on Israel. Some time ago, a Reuters article reported on conversations by the Israeli leadership: "Israel, widely believed to be the Middle East's only nuclear-armed power, has issued veiled warnings for years that it might attack Iran if international sanctions and diplomacy fail to curb Tehran's nuclear ambitions."[4] Netanyahu went on to say, "I think it's important to note that we (Israel) can't allow it to happen. Our clocks are ticking at a different pace. We're closer than the United States, we're more vulnerable, and therefore we'll have to address this question of whether to stop Iran before the United States does."[5] This kind of rhetoric is more than just saber rattling. A real threat is in the air that at some point will become an all-out war. In my imagination, I can see how a preemptive strike by Israel could ultimately lead to a war whereby Iran is joined with the allies mentioned in Ezekiel 38. Who knows? By the time you are reading these words, this attack may have already happened.

It is interesting to consider the current relationship between Russia and these five coalition nations. On October 17, 2007, the London Times printed a story carrying the following headline: Russia announces military alliance with Iran - Putin vows to help accelerate Iranian nuclear program and defend Iran against western aggression.[6] You will find that in the last five or so years, every one of the coalition nations has signed some kind of treaty with Russia. The only exception is Sudan, but they signed a very strong military alliance with Iran.[7]

All of this information is pointing to even greater unrest in the Middle East, which will lead to potential economic collapse in various world markets. I have already established that what happens in one part of the world greatly affects the rest of our global community. The difficulty facing us in the possible near future will lead many people to question God and lose small and great battles with our spiritual enemy. It is paramount that we pick up our shield of faith and hold onto the truth of God's Word. While the world slips into apparent chaos, we must by faith remember that God really is in control.

Our Enemy's Weapons

Let's go back to Ephesians 6:16: "In addition to all this, take up the shield of faith, with which you can extinguish all the flaming arrows of the evil one." This passage speaks briefly to the weapons of our spiritual enemy, the "flaming arrows of the evil one." God may have just been describing Satan's tactics as being like shooting a flaming arrow at us, but it is also possible God intended us to consider the danger of a flaming arrow. Thucydides, the ancient Greek writer, used the identical Greek expression to depict especially terrible arrows that were equipped to carry fire. The Romans developed a hollow tube with an attached spear head. The tubes were filled with some incendiary material so that when the arrow found its target, it would explode into flame.[8] We also know ancient armies sometimes shot arrows into the oncoming enemy that had been covered with pitch on one end and set afire.

The flaming arrows were shot from a distance and intended not only to cause damage from hitting their targets, but also to catch whatever they hit on fire. Using the imagery of flaming arrows could symbolize the real destruction that came from something like a secondary blast. The arrow caused damage, but the explosion or the fire that followed was the real threat. Whether or not God intended this inference to be considered, we cannot be sure, but we do know that Satan often works in that way. His initial assault may be painful or destructive, but it is the slow, burning result of his continued deviance that brings about significant devastation. For example, consider the demeaning consequences of lust. Lust alone can bring about shame and regret, but lust unchecked can eventually lead to outright adultery. As far as consequences and fallout from sin, the fiery destruction of adultery is far greater than the initial shot of the arrow of lust. We must be careful as we read this passage in the sixth chapter of Ephesians and not overlook the seriousness of Satan's weapons. We can see in the Bible, in history and in our own experiences that Satan's weapons are extremely dangerous.

We may have a tendency to overlook the danger and relegate the whole concept of spiritual warfare to fantasy writings, such as Tolkien's *Lord of the Rings* or Lewis' *Narnia.* However, we are told in 1 Peter 5:8-9, "Be of sober spirit, be on the alert. Your adversary, the devil, prowls around like a roaring lion, seeking someone to devour. But resist him, firm in your faith, knowing that the same experiences of suffering are being accomplished by your brethren who are in the world." The thought of a roaring lion can be chilling. I recently woke up to a screaming bobcat in my camp while in a National Forest in North Carolina. Unsettling does not adequately describe the feeling I had as I lay there trying to decide what to do. Fortunately, the big cat decided he might find more enjoyment elsewhere and moved on. Three possible reasons why a lion would roar have been determined by scientists. First, they roar to communicate with the rest of their pride. I'm not sure how that reason applies to this 1 Peter passage, but the next two reasons certainly do. Lions also roar to proclaim where their territory is located, and the roar can be heard for up to five miles. Satan is trying to claim territory or dominion over human beings all over the planet. His roar is a roar of domination and intimidation.

I feel a chill run up my spine when I consider the third reason for such a roar. A lion will sneak up on his prey and then "let out a roar that confuses the animal(s) and strikes fear into the lion's prey. The prey then cannot 'think' or react correctly out of fear and so is trapped and caught by the lion."[9] What a vivid picture of Satan's strategy to steal, kill, and destroy. He sneaks up on us and tries to bring confusion into our minds and emotions. If he can get people in a place where they are unable to think or react correctly, they can easily become trapped.

We typically think of Satan as the creature depicted on a late-night horror show, but the truth is he rarely shows up in such a frightening state. We are told in 2 Corinthians 11:14, "No wonder, for even Satan disguises himself as an angel of light." We know he is not an angel of light, but he masquerades around as such. He might come as a beautiful and scantily dressed woman or a prime opportunity to fatten one's bank account from the company funds. Regardless of how he looks in the heat of temptation, it is usually quite appealing. If the college coed saw Satan as the drunk lying in the street, she would never take the first drink at the frat party that led to a night of thoughtless debauchery. If the traveling business man saw the destruction that came to his wife and children because of his wandering eyes, he would never turn his hotel television channel to the pornographic movie or go with his buddies to the strip club in the seedy part of town. Do not get sucked into Satan's deceptions: he is dreadfully dangerous.

Satan's weapons are also deadly; he wants you to die – really die! He wants your soul for all of eternity. He will do all manner of things to discount the claims of the gospel and lead people to refuse the offer of salvation. He presents counter arguments to the truth of God's

Word. Consider the tenets of naturalism that claim we do not need God to be our creator because everything evolved naturally over time. The lie of Satan repeats, "You do not need God." The whole line of reasoning behind naturalism or humanism says human beings are self-actualized from within, insinuating that no need for a Savior exists. We must remind ourselves often that Satan wants to kill us for eternity. He wants our eternal home to be hell.

Because of Satan's disposition, his weapons are destructive. I do believe Satan prefers the slow burn to the all-out explosion. I once heard seminary professor Dr. Preston Nix say, "What usually looks like a blowout is really a slow leak," as he described the moral failures of Christians.[10] When we use the word "destructive," we typically think of the fallout from a tornado or hurricane not the crumbling of a house as a result of termites. Nevertheless, a house that takes five years to crumble because of termites is still just as destroyed as a house that disintegrated in a matter of seconds due to a tornado. I know that Satan's fiery arrows eventually bring greater destruction because of the long-term consequences and eventual fallout. For example, studies show that one-third of all people who were abused as children become abusive parents. While sin has its initial affect in the life of a child, in many cases, this sin continues in a cyclical way continuing to bring increasing amounts of pain to the next generation.[11]

We could say the arrows also represent lies Satan shoots into our minds. As these lies begin their slow burn, the lifelong consequences can be overwhelming. He whispers, "You will never amount to anything," and we slowly begin to see ourselves as having little to no value and write ourselves off as a failure. He says, "You are a spiritual failure who will never defeat this habit," and we accept our fate as a moral failure and give in to a lifestyle of spiritual defeat. Satan wants to destroy us and limit our spiritual effectiveness, and the only way we can overcome this fiery dart is through our shield of faith.

Picking Up the Shield of Faith

Whenever God led Paul to tell us to pick up our shield of faith as we step onto the battlefield of life, the imagery was crystal clear to the first century church. Roman soldiers had different shields they carried for varying purposes. One was a small, round shield that was beautifully decorated, and the soldier carried it in parades. It was called an *aspis*. The second was called a *thureos*, which comes from the Greek word that is translated "door." This shield was used in battle. The *thureos* was similar to a small door in size in that it was about four feet tall by two and a half feet wide, and it curved in on the sides. The soldiers could form a line by placing the shields side by side, thereby presenting a formidable target. Soldiers often soaked their shields in water in order to extinguish flaming arrows. Sometimes soldiers squatted and held their shields above them creating a ceiling of protection against incoming arrows or spears. It is this second kind of shield that God compared to the important piece of our spiritual armor called faith.[12] Our faith is for battle, not for show.

In seeking a definition of faith, we might consider Hebrews 11:1: "Now faith is confidence in what we hope for and assurance about what we do not see." As Christians, our confident hope is in a victorious Savior. Jesus' victory was seen not only at the empty tomb, but it will also be seen at His glorious appearing. Picking up our shield of faith means that we really do believe that Jesus is in control and will be victorious, and we act upon that belief. Putting on faith also means that we adjust our actions and our thoughts to this confident assurance we have in our hearts. I say we must adjust our thoughts because the intense spiritual battle begins in our minds before it ever expresses itself any other way. It is because of this reality that God warned us to defeat Satan on the battlefield of our minds first. Second Corinthians 10:3-5 addresses this truth:

> For though we live in the world, we do not wage war as the world does. The weapons we fight with are not the weapons of the world. On the contrary, they have divine power to demolish strongholds.

> We demolish arguments and every pretension that sets itself up against the knowledge of God, and we take captive every thought to make it obedient to Christ.

It is very difficult to defeat Satan in our actions if we have not first defeated him in our minds. It is a significant challenge to quietly trust God when everything seems to be coming apart all around us if we have not stopped the satanic, mental onslaught of the evil one who seeks to announce loudly our doom.

We can try to defeat Satan with our own prowess, clever tactics and stiff determination, but we will find our greatest weapon to be the Word of God. Jesus demonstrated this dependence upon Scripture when He was confronted by Satan in the wilderness. We can see in the fourth chapter of Matthew that Jesus quoted the Old Testament Scripture on three occasions to overcome Satan's advances. Picking up our shield of faith means we believe God's Word. We will actually find the Bible to be our primary tool to use in response to our faith and to build our faith. Romans 10:17 says, "So faith comes from hearing, and hearing by the word of Christ." We will not be able to pick up our shield if we do not know the Scripture. It is interesting how often we will find every piece of our spiritual armor connected to the Bible. The Bible is the content for the belt of truth, the revelation of Christ Who is the basis of our breastplate of righteousness, the explanation of the gospel of peace, the source of our faith, the assurance of our salvation, the strength behind the sword of the Spirit, and the foundation for our prayers of faith. It should not be surprising that throughout history, Satan has worked to discredit the Bible and lead people to discount it as a book of fairytales instead of as the inspired Word of God.

Not only is faith believing God's Word, but it is also trusting God's sovereignty. All throughout the Scripture, we see God referred to as "sovereign." Consider the words of the Psalmist: "For you have been my hope, Sovereign LORD, my confidence since my youth" (Psalm 71:5 - NIV). Sovereign means having "supreme power or authority"[13] It is essential that we acknowledge God's sovereignty in uncertain times. If the Rapture has not yet occurred when Russia and her coalition come down to fight against Israel, some unknowing believers will wonder why God has abandoned Israel and His church.

As Christians become increasingly pinpointed as the the objects of persecution, some will begin to think God is no longer in control. Just this week the news is reporting that thousands of Christians are being persecuted in Iraq by the radical group ISIS. I will never forget the visual I saw on the news of thousands of fleeing Christians climbing a mountain in an effort to escape the murderous intent of the Christian-hating, radical Muslims; and one of the precious saints was an elderly woman who had to use a walker. It is easy for us to be emotionally touched by this persecution, but right now, these atrocities are happening far away from us. One day, the physical persecution of Christians will be occurring in our own country. Real faith says that we trust God no matter what happens. Faith acknowledges that we do not have the capacity to understand everything, so we fully trust in the God Who is in control and Who certainly knows all things.

As a part of trusting God's sovereignty, real faith will always be confident in God's promises. Christians who have walked with the Lord through the years have learned to trust God's promises. Over time, we discover that God has never broken His promises, and He is not about to start doing so now. Peter wrote to encourage Christians enduring persecution with these words in 2 Peter 1:4: "He has granted to us His precious and magnificent promises, so that by them you may become partakers of the divine nature, having escaped the corruption that is in the world by lust." God says that through these promises, we actually participate in Christ's nature. Note how Peter was inspired to conclude this passage.

We escape corruption that is caused by evil desires when we believe and act upon the promises of God. God has given us many "very great and precious promises." For example, Hebrews 13:5 says, "Never will I leave you; never will I forsake you." There may be times leading up to the rapture of the church when Christians may feel abandoned by God, but we must hold on to the promise of Hebrews 13:5.

Jesus emphatically stated, "Never will I leave you…" When Jesus said "never," He means "never!" This promise will bring great comfort in the painful throws of a dark night when it seems like everything is coming apart. This truth means when we feel alone at the bedside of our dying mate, God has not abandoned us. When the pain of losing a child is so great that we do not realize God is beside us, we can trust in His presence anyway. And when we are being persecuted for our faith, we can hold on to God until the very end – even if it means giving our lives for the cause of Christ.

While it may be difficult for Americans to think about facing death because of our faith, many will be forced to do so during the last days. We are not as accustomed to this idea in the United States, but people die for their faith often in other places of the world. According to Italian sociologist and author Dr. Massimo Introvigne, "Christians are the most persecuted group in the world, with one Christian being killed out of religious discrimination every five minutes."[14] If you happen to be one sitting alone in a cell one day awaiting your execution, hold on to God because He has not abandoned you. At that time, you will be able to celebrate in the joy of knowing that within moments you will be seeing your Savior face to face, and you will have the great joy of hearing the One Who gave His life for you say, "Well done good and faithful servant."

Do you really believe the promises of God? Picking up the shield of faith means you believe what God says regardless of what is going on around you.

Faith Means Action

Faith also means that regardless of our circumstances, we always choose to be obedient to God's commands. We tend to view the word "faith" as a noun, but the New Testament believers saw it first and foremost as a verb. We think that you either have faith, or you do not have faith. You either defend your faith, or you lose your faith. Faith is seen primarily by twenty-first century Christians as something that can be dropped or picked up. If faith is only a noun, it is something that one acquires. Because we tend to think it can be an acquisition, it can become static and stale. Ministry leader Steven Argue pointed out that if it is just a noun, then once we receive it, we put it on a shelf. To many people, Christianity is only an experience they once had in their lives as a child that involved baptism, and since then it has made no difference how they live.[15]

Faith is seen in the New Testament as a noun, but many times it is described as a verb. Faith is really an action word. People do not just receive faith, they live it. If a person's faith is only a noun and not a verb, it is not the authentic faith of the Bible. Many people who think they are Christians will spend eternity in hell because they were led to believe faith is only an asset that can be turned on or leaned upon as needed, but it was not something that really impacted or altered their lives. Part of our "faithing" comes in the form of obedience to God's commands.

When we pick up the shield of faith, we are making conscious choices to express our faith actively by doing what God commands us to do. Obedience to God's commands will increasingly make Christians different from the rest of the world as sinful lifestyles around us become more pronounced. Unfortunately, our obedience to Christ may label us as intolerant or bigots or narrow-minded, which may be the basis of future persecution; nevertheless, real Christians will remain faithful allowing faith to be expressed by their actions. James 2:14 emphasizes this truth: "What good is it, my brothers and sisters, if someone claims to have faith but has no deeds? Can such faith save them?"

I am burdened by the fact that many people in our world today have a "faith" that does not show itself in deeds, and these people do not really know God's saving grace.

Without the shield of faith, we are helpless before a well-armed enemy who continues to shoot a barrage of burning arrows into the family of God. Faith will continue to be a critical part of our victorious Christian experience, and as the return of Christ draws closer, the need for a strong and active faith will increase. Our faith cannot be in ourselves or in our formulas or in anything other than Jesus Christ and His unfailing Word. Through the years, I have put my faith in some crazy things: thin ice, unraveling ropes, rickety bicycles, and untrustworthy people. It is time for the church of the Lord Jesus Christ to stand strong against the violent assault of the forces of hell with our shields of faith raised high. We must display a faith that is placed in the unwavering and unchanging Jesus Christ, and having done everything God has commanded us to do, we must stand firm against the forces of our mortal enemy.

CHAPTER NINE

The Helmet of Salvation

Some months ago, my family and I traveled to Charleston, South Carolina, for a wedding. There I had a momentary, startling experience. I have ridden motorcycles for many years of my life and am quite familiar with what is required in order to be a safe rider. As I walked down the street near The Battery, I looked up to see a man breeze by on his motorcycle, and to my temporary shock, I realized he was not wearing a helmet. It only took a moment for me to remember that South Carolina law does not require motorcycle riders to wear helmets. My next thought was really a question: Why wouldn't someone want to wear a helmet whether they were required to do so by law or not? A few years ago, I took a spill on my bike, and although I wasn't going very fast, my helmet may have saved my life. I've been accused of being hardheaded, but I'm quite confident that had I not been wearing a helmet, I would have been seriously hurt, if not killed. I wouldn't think about riding a motorcycle without a helmet. Common sense tells me that one little fall could be fatal if my head were not protected.

As Paul sat in his prison cell, he took note of the soldier's helmet that either sat on his head or rested on the floor beside him, and he thought of the essential nature of this important piece of armor. Even as a soldier would not go into battle without this critical piece of protection, a person should not step onto the battlefield of life without the essential experience of salvation. When I think about the metal helmet soldiers wear into battle, my thoughts center upon the function of the helmet and the necessary material needed for the helmet to accomplish its purpose.

The soldier's helmet was made of thick metal that was quite heavy. Because of the uncomfortable nature of the helmet, some type of cushion was placed inside in an attempt to help the soldier not have a continuous headache from the strain of wearing this protective covering. Not only were the helmets thick with metal, but also many times, metal pieces stretched down the sides of the soldiers' faces, like long metal sideburns providing additional protection. This piece of equipment had to be strong enough to withstand the blow of a battle axe or the sharp point of an enemy's arrow. This vital piece of armor was probably the last thing a soldier put on before going into battle, but it was definitely essential for survival.

It is interesting that Paul was led to compare salvation to a soldier's helmet. As God is directing us to be able to stand firm in the evil days, we must contemplate the significance of salvation being like a thick, protective covering to our heads. The first thing that comes to my mind is the fact that our head is the center of our thinking processes. It is our salvation that gives us clarity of mind as we ward off the lies and deceit of our enemy. Satan weakens the church of Jesus Christ by causing us to question the truth of God's Word and to doubt the promise of God's constant presence in our lives. I've mentioned previously that our minds are the initial battlefield, and it is the confidence of our salvation through Christ that gives us clarity as we sift through the mental attacks that could weaken our resolve.

Confronting Deception

It should not surprise us that Jesus warned of deception as a sign of His return. When the disciples asked Jesus about the signs of His second coming, Jesus told them six different times that great deception would be commonplace. His very first statement to answer the disciples' question was a warning about the coming deception: "See to it that no one misleads you" (Matthew 24:4). Again, this warning should not surprise us because we know that Satan is our archenemy, and he is called a liar in the Scripture.

Jesus addressed a group of Jewish people in John 8:44 with some thoughts about Satan's character: "You are of your father the devil, and you want to do the desires of your father. He was a murderer from the beginning and does not stand in the truth because there is no truth in him. Whenever he speaks a lie, he speaks from his own nature, for he is a liar and the father of lies." Jesus said truth does not coexist with Satan, and his very nature consistently speaks lies. Satan is incapable of speaking truth, and his deception is a normal experience in the spiritual battles we face every day. From the warnings of Matthew 24, Jesus indicates the deception will increase as the end draws closer.

Anticipating a Global Government

The Bible reveals that a world leader will come to power and lead the world through a global government during the Tribulation Period. While we do not know everything about this world leader, we do know that his leadership will be filled with deception. We could surmise this point first by the fact that he will be Satan's pawn, and Satan's typical mode of operation is deception. I have also tried to imagine how all of the leaders of the sovereign nations of our world will willingly give up the countries to this world leader, and several possible thoughts have come to my mind.

It is possible the world will ultimately be in such chaos that leaders will gladly turn their nations over to a world leader out of sheer desperation. I do think global chaos will play into this decision, but the thing that will make a one-world government appear to be a good idea will be some sort of deception by the evil one. I discussed the significance of the statue in Nebuchadnezzar's dream and pointed out the picture of the final, one-world government represented by the statue's feet. Though the ten toes of the statue are thought to represent ten world regions led by ten world leaders, their leadership is obviously under the direction of, or superseded by, one primary leader. In another dream the Lord gave Daniel, God spoke more specifically about this world leader. Consider God's revelation to the prophet in Daniel 7:7-8, 24-25:

> After this I kept looking in the night visions, and behold, a fourth beast, dreadful and terrifying and extremely strong; and it had large iron teeth. It devoured and crushed and trampled down the remainder with its feet; and it was different from all the beasts that were before it, and it had ten horns. While I was contemplating the horns, behold, another horn, a little one, came up among them, and three of the first horns were pulled out by the roots before it; and behold, this horn possessed eyes like the eyes of a man and a mouth uttering great boasts…As for the ten horns, out of this kingdom ten kings will arise; and another will arise after them, and he will be different from the previous ones and will subdue three kings. 'He will speak out against the Most High and wear down the saints of the Highest One, and he will intend to make alterations in times and in law; and they will be given into his hand for a time, times, and half a time.

It is obvious in Daniel's dream that this strong, world leader will be preceded by an early attempt to consolidate the world into a single government under the direction of the ten leaders. Let me emphasize this truth again: the ten leaders will come to power *before* the Antichrist is revealed. The Antichrist will be the king who "will arise after them." Somehow, the Antichrist will overthrow three of the world leaders and gain the respect and submission of the remaining seven leaders. I have no doubt in my mind that great deception will be used to orchestrate the one-world government and to secure control of the remaining seven leaders.

If the rapture of the church is to be in my lifetime, which I think is very possible, then these ten world leaders are alive, and efforts may be underway now to secure this global, political picture. If the ten leaders are currently situated in the wings of this coming global drama, it is easy to assume that even the Antichrist is alive and well on the planet as I am penning these words. He may be a little boy or he may be working quietly in some small government, but Satan could be working to set the stage for this final act.

What will the Antichrist Be Like?

Daniel's prophecy provides us several important facts we need to know about the Antichrist:

- He will be a strong, charismatic leader. Daniel 7:20 refers to the Antichrist as being "the horn that looked more imposing than the others and that had eyes and a mouth that spoke boastfully."
- Though seemingly insignificant, he will wield great power. Daniel 7:8 speaks of his surprising power: "While I was contemplating the horns, behold, another horn, a little one, came up among them, and three of the first horns were pulled out by the roots before it; and behold, this horn possessed eyes like the eyes of a man and a mouth uttering great boasts."
- He will speak blasphemy against God and persecute Christians. While all Christians will be taken up in the rapture, the Bible does indicate people will be saved during the Tribulation Period. It is reasonable to think this persecution will not wait until after the rapture, but rather will begin long before the church is "caught up to meet the Lord in the air." Daniel 7:25 says, "He will speak out against the Most High and wear down the saints of the Highest One, and he will intend to make alterations in times and in law; and they will be given into his hand for a time, times, and half a time."

  The Apostle John also spoke of this future persecution in Revelation 13:5-8:

> There was given to him a mouth speaking arrogant words and blasphemies, and authority to act for forty-two months was given to him. And he opened his mouth in blasphemies against God, to blaspheme His name and His tabernacle, *that is*, those who dwell in heaven. It was also given to him to make war with the saints and to overcome them, and authority over every tribe and people and tongue and nation was given to him. All who dwell on the earth will worship him, *everyone* whose name has not been written from the foundation of the world in the book of life of the Lamb who has been slain.

- He will be empowered by Satan. In Revelation 13:3-4, the Antichrist is referred to as "the beast": "And the whole earth was amazed and followed after the beast; they worshiped the dragon because he gave his authority to the beast; and they worshiped the beast, saying, 'Who is like the beast, and who is able to wage war with him?'"
- According to Revelation 13:16-18, he will be worshiped and will require people to be marked. This marking will happen during the Tribulation Period and will have eternal consequences for those who take the number:

> And he causes all, the small and the great, and the rich and the poor, and the free men and the slaves, to be given a mark on their right hand or on their forehead, and *he provides* that no one will be able to buy or to sell, except the one who has the mark, *either* the name of the beast or the number of his name. Here is wisdom. Let him who has understanding calculate the number of the beast, for the number is that of a man; and his number is six hundred and sixty-six.

- He will be defeated by Jesus Christ. Revelation 19:11-16 and 19-20 speaks of the great war between Jesus and the Antichrist where Jesus, the One called "Faithful and True," will throw the Antichrist and the false prophet into the lake of fire. This passage refers to the Antichrist as having "deceived those who had received the mark of the beast."

In a way, I find it hard to imagine the entire world allowing one man to take over the global helm, but at the same time, I have been amazed to see people willingly pledge themselves to rogue leaders in the past. I only need to mention a few names like Adolf Hitler, Benito Mussolini, or even Jim Jones in Guyana in order to acknowledge that people are surprisingly ready to give up everything to follow a convincing leader. Paul-Henri Spaak served as the first president of the United Nations General Assembly, was the former prime minister of Belgium, served as the first president of the European Parliament, and was the former secretary general of NATO. It is reported that he made this amazing declaration of the world's need for a strong, global leader: "We do not need another committee. We have too many already. What we want is a man of sufficient stature to hold the allegiance of all people, and to lift us out of the economic morass into which we are sinking. Send us such a man and be he god or devil, we will receive him."[1]

The Antichrist *is* coming, and the events that will make his rule inevitable will begin to take place long before the Tribulation Period begins. Because of this anticipated global challenge, it is critical that Christians put on the helmet of salvation daily. It would be easy to see this piece of armor as simply a reminder of how important it is for everyone to become a Christian, but I think the helmet of salvation points to more than just people repenting of their sins and trusting Jesus as Savior. If we are going to regularly put on the helmet of salvation, we must understand the full expression of salvation and know that we experience spiritual victory in different ways at the various levels of our Christian journey.[2]

The Past Tense of Salvation

If you are a Christian, you had an initial experience with Christ whereby you were saved from the penalty of sin. We can think of this aspect of our salvation as the past tense. I can refer to my own experience by saying that when I was seven-years-old, I repented of my sin and trusted Jesus as my Savior. At that moment, the Lord Jesus forgave me of my sin and came to live in my life. Though I learned more about what it meant to be a Christian as I grew in my faith, I will always look back to that Sunday night in my bedroom when I knelt beside my bed with my parents and asked Jesus to forgive me for my sin and come into my life. At that moment, my sins were forgiven, and I became a part of God's family. Because of God's grace, the penalty of my sin was transferred to Jesus, for His death became my payment for salvation. Peter spoke of this tense of salvation in the early words of his first letter: "Blessed be the God and Father of our Lord Jesus Christ, who according to His great mercy has caused us to be born again to a living hope through the resurrection of Jesus Christ from the dead" (1 Peter 1:3).

Putting on the helmet of salvation calls us to remember often the sacrifice Christ made on our behalf, thereby making forgiveness possible for us. I wrote earlier of Satan's deceptive methods whereby he will try to trip us up and make us spiritually ineffective. One tool he uses often is the tool of doubt. It does not take too much creativity to be able to see how ineffective we can become in our spiritual lives and in the battle being waged for the souls of mankind if we are constantly doubting our salvation. While it is important for people not to develop a false security in an inauthentic faith, it is equally important that we have a strong confidence in God's grace if our faith is the real thing. I must emphasize that I am convinced many people who call themselves Christians are actually lost.

People seek salvation in many ways other than through Jesus Christ. Most people think they are going to heaven because of good works, even though the Bible clearly says it is not by works of righteousness (Titus 3:5). I have always been amazed at the number of people who search for an experience sometime in their distant past whereby they prayed a prayer thinking the magic words had been spoken resulting in their eternal security. I have performed numerous funerals over the years where a family member of the deceased would try to convince me their loved one was in heaven because of a "prayer" spoken as a child followed by a watery baptism. The problem is often that this supposed dead saint never lived the Christian life.

I do not want to give anyone a false security. Praying a prayer does not make someone a Christian. You can say words all day long with the only result being a hoarse voice and a sore throat. Please understand this truth: the real evidence of an authentic faith is a changed life! Hell will be filled with people who lived right, prayed a prayer, and even went to church. With that said, it is also important to emphasize that once you are a Christian, Satan works hard to plant seeds of doubt in your mind. Putting on the helmet of salvation means that we look back in our lives and know that our repentance was real and our faith is authentic. This piece of armor underscores that we have settled in our minds that we are indeed children of God and not waffle back and forth as Satan whispers confusing thoughts into our minds. In these days, we need a strong army of spiritual soldiers to stand against Satan and his cronies. We do not need to be weakened by continuous doubt regarding our faith. Settle the issue and stand strong and secure in God's grace.

The Present Tense of Salvation

Salvation also has a present tense. While I can look back to when I was a child and say with biblical confidence that I *was* saved from the penalty of sin, I can also look at my life today and say with equal assurance that I *am being* saved from the power of sin. Peter also addressed this concept briefly in 1 Peter 1:2 when he referred to the "sanctifying work of the Spirit." It was this present tense aspect of our salvation that Paul addressed as he wrote to the church at Corinth: "For the word of the cross is foolishness to those who are perishing, but to us who are being saved it is the power of God" (1 Corinthians 1:18).

As the end of time draws ever closer, Satan seems to be gaining increasingly more control of humanity, thereby unleashing sin in unbelievable ways. Temptations abound today that were not even considered a few years ago. The possibility of viewing shameful websites with the click of a few keys on our computers is an ever present danger to any Christian. The potential for moral failure is very real for every believer as standards for morality are constantly declining. Even people who are considered spiritual leaders are sometimes acceding immorality as acceptable, thereby making it even more challenging for steadfast Christians to maintain their commitment to moral purity.

In the past, television promoted not only positive values, but also a healthy worldview. Today, television has become a dangerous tool in the hands of the deceiver as he uses the flash of Hollywood to lead susceptible minds down a path that ultimately denies the existence of God. We need a present tense salvation that is constantly at work in our hearts giving us strength, discernment, and wisdom in overcoming the influences of hell.

Earlier, I mentioned 2 Corinthians 10:3-5: "For though we walk in the flesh, we do not war according to the flesh, for the weapons of our warfare are not of the flesh, but divinely powerful for the destruction of fortresses. We are destroying speculations and every lofty thing raised up against the knowledge of God, and we are taking every thought captive to the obedience of Christ." This passage points to the present tense nature of our salvation. It describes the daily battle as the process of destroying "fortresses." The context indicates these strongholds, or enemy outposts, are not physical but mental. They are not some literal fort of the enemy made up of stone and mortar, but rather they are in our minds. The fifth verse says, "We are destroying speculations."

The present tense nature of that passage indicates that this process is an ongoing aspect of our salvation, and the "speculations" seem to be synonymous with "fortresses." Satan erects a number of fortresses, but at least one of them is in our minds. This particular Greek word that is translated "speculations" in the NASB is only used twice in the

New Testament (here and in Romans 2:15 where it is translated "thoughts"). This word usage points to the fact that these strongholds are often found on the battlefield of our minds, and they must be pulled down. This fortress is like a mental outpost for the enemy where he can gain portions of our minds. For example, Satan may use the fortress of past failures or childhood abuse to make you feel like a worthless failure. He might be able to make you question your value to God, thereby rendering you weak and ineffective in the spiritual battle. Salvation is a daily experience as we defeat Satan in his constant efforts to trip us up in our walk with Christ.

As time draws closer to Christ's return, it is important that Christians not fall prey to Satan's lies that say they cannot share their faith with others because of their past failures. He uses the strongholds of fear and intimidation to keep Christians silent, and those who desperately need to hear the gospel end up going to a Christless eternity because of the effectiveness of Satan's outpost in their minds. As sin increases and time grows short, Christians must be active in ministry and evangelism and make the most of every opportunity the Lord gives us to stand for Him.

Part of our present tense salvation means that we are regularly being equipped for our daily victories. We understand that victorious Christian living is experienced one day at a time. While the past tense concept of our salvation focuses on being made *right* with Christ, the present tense idea of our salvation focuses on being made *like* Christ. Paul addressed this idea in 2 Corinthians 3:18: "But we all, with unveiled face, beholding as in a mirror the glory of the Lord, are being transformed into the same image from glory to glory, just as from the Lord, the Spirit." Our daily victory over sin comes as we allow God to transform our thinking and our actions so that our lives reflect the character and mission of Jesus Christ. We live now in a time where those reflecting the character of Christ stand out significantly from those who do not know Christ. This distinction will only increase as the return of Christ draws nearer. Paul warned Timothy about these times in 2 Timothy 3:1-5:

> But realize this, that in the last days difficult times will come. For men will be lovers of self, lovers of money, boastful, arrogant, revilers, disobedient to parents, ungrateful, unholy, unloving, irreconcilable, malicious gossips, without self-control, brutal, haters of good, treacherous, reckless, conceited, lovers of pleasure rather than lovers of God, holding to a form of godliness, although they have denied its power; Avoid such men as these.

If we are going to put on the helmet of salvation, it means we are surrendering daily to God's construction project in our lives whereby we are made more and more like His Son. It means that while Satan is filling our minds full of lies, and the world is calling wrong right and right wrong, we keep doing the right thing every day. It really is about knowing what to do and doing it. It is about making choices every day to take every thought captive, to surrender our will to the will of God, to pledge our way to the way of God, and to yield our weakness to the strength of God. God told us in Philippians 2:12-13, "So then, my beloved, just as you have always obeyed, not as in my presence only, but now much more in my absence, work out your salvation with fear and trembling; for it is God who is at work in you, both to will and to work for His good pleasure."

The Future Tense of Salvation

A future tense of our salvation exists that must be connected to this helmet, for God tells us to anticipate the completion of our salvation where we will be rescued from the presence of sin. God inspired Peter to refer to believers as being "protected by the power of God through faith for a salvation ready to be revealed in the last time" (1 Peter 1:5). This future tense is critical for us as we move forward into uncertain days because we are bound to face times of great difficulty and discouragement. It is our secure hope in God's promised fulfillment and completion of our salvation that will give us the strength and the grace to hold on and continue to be faithful.

Paul even wrote to the Thessalonians to encourage one another with the reminder that Jesus will one day rapture His church.[3] It is obvious by Paul's words that he anticipates the church going through difficult times and will need to be encouraged. It is reassuring to be reminded that our difficulties are only temporary. God has an eternal plan, and we will soon be taken out of this world. Because we are sure to face greater persecution in the future and living out our faith will become exceedingly difficult, we can find great hope in Christ's promised return. Even death for Christ's sake can be embraced with great joy because we will know it is only a "light and momentary affliction" that Paul said "is producing for us an eternal weight of glory far beyond all comparison, while we look not at the things which are seen, but at the things which are not seen; for the things which are seen are temporal, but the things which are not seen are eternal" (2 Corinthians 4:17-18).

Most English translations begin verse seventeen of Ephesians chapter six with the word "take." In verse thirteen, we are told to take up the full armor of God, and in verse sixteen we are told to take up the shield of faith. The Greek word that is translated as "take" in verse seventeen is a totally different word. It actually means "receive." "Take" is an action term giving power and initiative to the one doing the acting while the action in the word "receive" is more passive as one responds to someone else whose actions are impacting him or her. It is very significant that we understand this basic theological truth regarding our salvation: God is always the initiator. Salvation was God's idea from the beginning, and nothing can be done to initiate our own salvation. It stems from God's amazing grace and merciful act whereby He offered Himself on a cross for the sins of the world. Our response to "so great a salvation" is simply to receive it (Hebrews 2:3). We are receiving what God has made possible to all of humanity by surrendering our lives to the control of Jesus Christ. As we put on this helmet of salvation, we must acknowledge we can only put it on because God first offered it.

Putting on the helmet of salvation means we understand and embrace every aspect of our salvation: past, present, and future. The battle for our souls was certainly won in the past as the truth of the cross impacted our hearts, thereby leading us to repentance and faith. The daily battle over sin, however, is won moment by moment as we walk freshly in the power and presence of the Holy Spirit of God holding on to the truth of His Word and the hope of His return. This kind of helmet, our salvation, will withstand any kind of hammering the enemy may bring our way not only ushering us into God's presence and our eternal home, but also shining forth the light of Jesus Christ in us so brightly that all will know that Jesus Christ is indeed the Light of the World.

CHAPTER TEN

The Sword of the Spirit

The best offense is a good defense, or is it the other way around? I played football in high school, and I remember hearing that phrase over and over. Of course I think the guy I heard it from the most may have been the defensive coordinator. I suppose that's kind of like the boys' playground chant in second grade: boys rule – girls drool. I'm sure the girls had a chant too; I was just not privy to it. Although football is now only something I enjoy on T.V. or in the front yard with my children, I know something now that was surely tucked back in my mind during my youth: you can't win the game without an offense *and* a defense. Both are essential.

When we consider the next piece of spiritual armor God inspired Paul to include in his list, I don't think we can just call it an offensive weapon. As soon as I imagine a Roman soldier pursuing the enemy who is in retreat (offense), I also see that same enemy turning and swinging his sword at his pursuer (defense). The sword in the Roman soldier's hand that was at first offensive, advancing the cause of his army, suddenly becomes a defensive weapon as he parries the blow of his once retreating attacker. The best offense is a good defense, and in this case, the sword is both. Paul told the Christians, "To take the helmet of salvation and the sword of the Spirit, which is the Word of God" (Ephesians 6:17). It seems to me the helmet of salvation must have been thought of as a defensive tool. The sword, however, must be viewed in a slightly different way. You will see in the discussion that follows that we need God's Word for both advancing the cause of Christ as well as for defending ourselves against our spiritual enemy.

The first word of verse seventeen is "take." The only problem with translating the Greek word *dekomai*, which is the root form of the word used in this verse as "take," is that it is really the word "receive," as I wrote about in the previous chapter. It is easier for me to attach the word "receive" to the helmet of salvation than it is to connect it to the sword of the Spirit. I am more of an action guy and really like the image of me grabbing my sword and demolishing my enemy like I am a super hero or something. Unfortunately, or really fortunately, that is not how spiritual victory works. Whether I have strong muscles or whether they have atrophied from years of disuse, God is the initiator. Even as He did the acting for our salvation, taking a step toward us before we ever even considered taking a step toward Him, He also does the speaking. We do not bravely jerk out our sword fearlessly in the presence of our snarling enemy. We receive the sword from the Lord. He draws the sword in the presence of our enemy and hands it to us. It is true that we have to swing it, but we will always find God taking the first step. We are not really taking up the Word of God as much as we are receiving it. This comment may seem like a small distinction, but it is really not.

We live in a day in which our secular world has worked hard to remove our need for God. We applaud self-made men and women. We cheer when we hear of people pulling themselves up by their boot straps and trudging forward into the challenges of the day. We love the underdogs who win against all odds because of their perseverance and ingenuity. Our secular world doesn't need God for creation because of its belief in evolution. Some people feel as if they do not need God for provision because they have government welfare, while others do not need God for His law because they have just made up their own. Most people do not like to think of themselves as helpless, weak, or needy. They prefer to see themselves as independent, strong, and creative.

I too like to fix my own problems and fight my own battles. The only problem with this thinking is that it breeds nothing but defeat. We must remember that we are not doing hand-to-hand combat with human beings, which would be tough enough, but rather we are fighting against the hosts of hell! We are not equipped to fight these kinds of battles, and if God doesn't provide us the sword, our puny little pieces of picnic plastic will suddenly pale in comparison to the three foot long piece of sharpened metal Satan is swinging at our heads. As we consider this piece of armor, let's keep in mind that God is the one offering us His Word. He is speaking to us, and we are only required to receive His truth. We'll talk more about what it really means to receive God's Word later in the chapter, but right now, let's look at the remaining parts of Ephesians 6:17.

We are told to take (receive) the sword of the Spirit. While it was hard to imagine the soldier having his shield in the prison cell with Paul, it is not hard for us to imagine the guard having his sword. I would think a soldier's sword was more like his best friend than a tool of battle. I have read of ancient soldiers being so attached to their swords that they would name them. Consider the legendary sword of King Arthur, Excalibur, or Charlemagne's sword, Joyeuse. The Roman soldier was surely always armed and may have even kept his hand on the hilt of his sword, even when he slept. As the guard sat, paced, or dozed, Paul probably noticed the detail of this implement of death.

The Soldier's Sword

Roman soldiers carried one of several different kinds of swords. In the early days of the Roman Empire, the soldier carried a long sword called a *gladius*. It was referred to as a "two-handed" sword because of its size. While a blow from a *gladius* could surely be lethal, only one side of the sword had a sharpened edge. I remember seeing movies depicting ancient battles and watching soldiers swing these huge pieces of metal. A huge, heavy sword is probably the kind of weapon King

David carried into battle, although David's may have even been longer. How anyone lived is beyond me, but I think one can readily see the problem with this kind of sword. While one side was certainly lethal, the other side was not. Because of its huge and heavy size, I'm sure accuracy declined as the battle waged on. While the mere size of this sword would have been intimidating, its lack of effectiveness caused it to be replaced by a smaller, more effective weapon.[1]

The second and more preferred sword was one that was about seventeen inches long, and it was copied from a similar one carried by the Carthaginians, who defeated the Romans in the early stages of the Punic Wars (3rd – 2nd Century BC). While this sword was still only single-edged, it did have a sharp point making it effective from two different vantage points. The Romans probably did not see this sword as a different kind of *gladius*, but rather as an updated version.

Another type of sword the Roman soldier would have carried into battle was a short sword that would appear to us to be more like a dagger. It was referred to as a *pugio*.[2] This sword, or dagger, was carried hidden away in a scabbard and was used for up close fighting. The Cavalry used an even longer sword (around thirty inches or so) that was useful for thrusting toward the enemy from a galloping horse. While all of these weapons had their places, it was the fifth sword to which Paul referred in this Ephesians passage.

The word Paul chose in Ephesians 6:17 was not the one for the *gladius* or the *pugio*. This word came from the Greek word *machaira*, and it referred to a sharp, double-edged sword that was a little longer than the *gladius* but was curved on the tip. The double-edge obviously made the sword quite dangerous because it could cut both ways. The curved tip made the sword extremely deadly, for it would not only stab the enemy, but also it disemboweled him as it was turned. While that imagery is a gruesome thought, the Romans didn't play when it came to battle. We can learn from that mentality as we think about how serious our spiritual battles are. A first century soldier had the mentality of "kill or be killed." We must have similar thinking every day as we step on the battlefield of life. Satan doesn't play, and nor should we.

Let's think for a few minutes about this sword of the Spirit. Another interesting fact about the Roman sword is that it was altered based upon the typical terrain that might define a soldier's battlefield. I found this idea interesting. Although the length of the soldiers' swords varied, the conditions of the battlefield determined the particular form of the weapon. Though God's Word doesn't change, different passages are given to us for different applications. In one moment of temptation, we may need a long sword, and at other times, the shorter sword will be more suitable. I think we are hard pressed to take this illustration any further, but suffice it to say that God's Word has different applications for different circumstances. Now the question is, how do we know which application is for which circumstance?

Understanding the Sword of the Spirit

Notice that this weapon is called the "sword of the Spirit." The word "of" could denote possession or source. The sword could belong to the Holy Spirit of God, or it could come from Him. Either way, the sword is not ours to begin with. While we do need to develop skill in knowing how to use the sword in battle, it is the Holy Spirit's job to tell us which particular application of the sword we are to use. I tried to think of an illustration of this truth and had a thought that might give us some clarity. I'm not really much of a golfer now, though I played a good bit in my youth. I could never be good enough to play on the pro tour or even really compete in any kind of tournament, but some people play this game for a living. Can you imagine hitting a little white ball around a finely, manicured lawn for a paycheck?

If you have ever watched professional golfers, you know they do not play the game alone. Every golfer has a caddy. The caddy's job is not only to carry the clubs around so the professional golfer can remain as fresh as possible for the next shot, but also to recommend clubs to the golfer. Now, our illustration breaks down here a little. A golfer does not become a pro without knowing which club to use, so the caddy's suggestion is just that – a suggestion. God's Holy Spirit is walking around life with us, and when we engage in battle, He knows exactly which scripture to pull out of the bag that will help us to keep the ball in play. We defeat the enemy because the sword belongs to God and comes from Him. He hands us the exact sword for the moment, and we swing away.

As far as which of the soldier's swords God had in mind, we can make that determination by looking at Hebrews 4:12-13:

> For the word of God is living and active and sharper than any two-edged sword, and piercing as far as the division of soul and spirit, of both joints and marrow, and able to judge the thoughts and intentions of the heart. And there is no creature hidden from His sight, but all things are open and laid bare to the eyes of Him with whom we have to do.

God's Word is even sharper than the typical double-edged sword of the Roman soldier. I'm sure soldiers prided themselves on how sharp their swords were kept, but God says His Word is even sharper. When I think about running out onto the battlefield, I'm sure they would much rather have had a sharp sword than a dull one. While it might be a little disgusting to take this concept too far, a sharp sword will do a lot more damage and require a lot less energy. If you think about it, not only does the sword belong to the Lord, but also the battle belongs to Him as well. When we depend upon the Lord, we find renewed energy that comes from His indwelling Spirit. It cuts deep and defeats our enemy, and the truth is that God does all the work if we let Him. It is the double-edged sword of the Spirit.

Consider another thought connected to the Hebrews 4:12-13 passage. Notice that it says, "It penetrates even to dividing soul and spirit, joints and marrow; it judges the thoughts and attitudes of the heart." While we may be thinking about the enemy being "penetrated" by this sharp weapon, God's sword also penetrates our own hearts. It helps us to see ourselves as we really are, thereby making us a better soldier for battle. It says, "Everything is uncovered and laid bare before the eyes of Him to whom we must give account." While we may try to hide our actions or motives from God, others, and even ourselves, the Word of God exposes those hidden things and labels them with truth. For example, we may fall into sin, and in an effort to make ourselves feel better about our particular vice, we may label it something else. If we can't label it something other than sin, we may blame someone else for our problems. God's Word will slice through all of the self-deception and call our excuses what they are. Christian soldiers cannot stand firm on the battlefield unless they are spiritually trim and fit. God's Word helps us in that process.

Grasping the Word of God

Let's look at the second part of the Ephesians 6:17 passage. We are told to "take (receive)…the sword of the Spirit, which is the word of God." Imagine yourself to be Aristarchus, Paul's prison mate, and you are having a little chat with the great Apostle about this spiritual concept. To what do you think Paul is referring when he calls the sword of the Spirit the "Word of God?" Honestly, when I think about the Word of God, I think about the sixty-six books bound in leather I refer to as my Bible. I think about my Bible as my sword. Now, I realize God is not telling me to use my Bible as a weapon, though I've had one or two through the years that could have done some damage. It is obviously the words of Scripture between the bindings that contain spiritual power used for tearing down strongholds.

Now, let's go back to our imaginary conversation between Paul and Aristarchus. When Paul mentioned the Word of God, do you suppose Aristarchus was thinking about written words that were contained in a scroll? The answer is no. Paul could have used one of two different Greek terms that would have ended up in our English translation as "word." The most common Greek term that is translated "word" is the Greek word "logos." For example, John 1:1 says, "In the beginning was the word (logos), and the word (logos) was with God, and the word (logos) was God." The Holman Illustrated Bible Dictionary gave a thorough explanation of "the Greek word *logos* ("word"): "An explanation or reason for something otherwise meaningless. *Logos* has a variety of uses, depending on context. With regard to language or grammar, *logos* can mean 'sentence' or 'statement,' while regarding logic or knowledge, it can mean 'reason,' 'explanation,' 'science,' or 'formula.'"[3]

The idea of *logos* is communication. It is the complete expression of a thought or concept. To say that Jesus Christ is the Word Who was God is to say He is the complete communication of God to the world.

The only problem is that back in our imaginary conversation between Paul and Aristarchus, Paul didn't use the word *logos* when he told his cellmate to "receive the sword of the Spirit, which is the Word of God." He used *rhema*! It is obviously a totally different Greek word with a very different meaning. While *logos* is communication and the full expression of something through words and sentences or some other means of expression, *rhema* is simply spoken words. While the sword of the Spirit is certainly influenced by the written Word of God, the Bible, the sword to which Paul was referring was the spoken Word of God!

I am a concrete person, and the written Word is an easy concept to grasp. In this twenty-first century world, the spoken Word of God seems to be a little subjective, and some people think it is reserved for the Old Testament prophets. Since we have moved into the modern age with cell phones and Internet, maybe the spoken Word is not as prevalent. If this statement is true, then another question may come to our minds: Are we supposed to leave the sword of the Spirit home when we go into spiritual battle? The answer is a resounding *no*!

Hearing God Speak

Does God still speak today? Many times when I think of God speaking to people today, I picture the television preacher working to pump his audience for a little more money by holding his hand upon his forehead and telling his viewers that God is giving him a message. I'm not against television preachers. Come to think of it, I've been one before, but I do know charlatans can be found who use ministry for their own profit. I'm afraid the abuse of "God speaking" has created doubt in many minds, and when we hear someone say, "God spoke to me," we immediately write them off as wacky. The first question might be "Can God still speak today?" The answer has to be a quick yes. Is God limited? Can He not do anything He wants to do? Certainly God can speak, but maybe the correct question would be "Does God still speak today?" We know He certainly spoke to Moses, Joshua, David, Isaiah, Peter, and Paul. Of course, those guys lived over 2,000 years ago, but should that fact make modern day claims of God speaking suspect?

I have no doubt that God speaks today in a variety of ways. Author Henry Blackaby agrees and made this startling comment: "If the Christian does not know when God is speaking, he is in trouble at the heart of his Christian life!"[4] When I first read this statement years ago, it made me stop and suck in a deep breath. Once I got over the boldness of the statement, I had to agree that Blackaby was dead on right. We must hear God speak today, or we do not know the direction we are to go. If we cannot hear God speak, we do not have the ability to discern right from wrong. If we are dependent upon our own perspective and interpretations, I don't think we even have a fifty percent chance of getting it right. Professor Dallas Willard addressed the challenge of this concept:

> Hearing God? A daring idea, some would say – presumptuous and even dangerous. But what if we are made for it? What if the human system simply will not function properly without it? There are good reasons to think it will not. The fine texture as well as the grand movements of life show the need. Is it not, in fact, more presumptuous and dangerous to undertake human existence without hearing God?[5]

While hearing God speak appears to be "presumptuous and even dangerous," I think we will see through this discussion that it is also essential.

Think back to the Hebrews 4:12 passage we looked at above. Notice it says that the Word of God is "alive." In other words, God's Word is not some stagnant, aging piece of archaic manuscript that has no relevance to a twenty-first century world. It is a living expression of God's truth that always finds fresh application to our modern lives. If God does not speak, then how does God's Word penetrate to divide soul and spirit, joints and marrow? How does it judge the thoughts and attitudes of our hearts? It must be more than just terms on a piece of paper held together by glue and leather.

Consider the words of the Psalmist in Psalm 143:10: "Teach me to do your will, for you are my God; may your good Spirit lead me on level ground." If God does not speak today, how will He teach us to do His will? How does God's good Spirit lead us on level ground? I think you can see as you turn through the pages of Scripture that if God does not speak today, many portions of the Bible must be torn out. Maybe we can, however, wonder what God's voice is like and how does He exactly speak to us.

How Does God Speak?

First, when God speaks, He speaks out of the context of our relationship with Him. In the Bible, we find that God wants us to "know" Him. Consider Paul's passionate declaration in Philippians 3:10: "That I may know Him and the power of His resurrection and the fellowship of His sufferings, being conformed to His death…" Paul stated clearly that he wanted the Ephesians "to know the love of Christ which surpasses knowledge" (Ephesians 3:19).

This word *know* means more than just a gathering of data that increases our intellectual understanding of a subject. Consider the King James Version of the Old Testament concept that said, "And Adam knew Eve his wife; and she conceived, and bare Cain." (Genesis 4:1 - KJV). Adam's knowledge of Eve was a lot more than just intellectual. The Bible concept of knowing includes the idea of experiencing. God wants us to experience Him through a growing, vibrant relationship whereby we are doing life together. While God can certainly speak to someone with whom He has no relationship (consider the Apostle Paul as exhibit A), our relationship with Him certainly opens us up to understand and receive His communications. Because of my relationship with my wife, I can hear her speak to me without her even having to open her mouth. It might be a nod or a smile. It could come through raised eyebrows or just through how I know she thinks. Because of our relationship with Christ, we will be more tuned in when He does speak.

Another truth I should add to this discussion is that when God does speak to us, His first desire is to strengthen our relationship with Him. He really does want us to know Him. At times in my life, I thought I really needed to hear God speak about a certain issue, but I found His focus seemed to be on our relationship while my focus was on getting an answer about a particular decision. One day, it occurred to me that nothing is more important than my relationship with God. The truth is that God gives answers to our questions as they are needed, but it is our relationship that is most important.

Second, when God speaks, He speaks out of the context of His revelation. While God's revelation speaks loudly, God reveals Himself in more than just one way. For example, we may learn of God's vastness by studying the expanse of space. We may learn of God's creativity in a biology class where we discover the complexity of the human body. Creation is a vivid revelation of the person and power of our Creator. This general type of revelation provides for us a constant reverberation of the vocal chords of the Almighty. He is always speaking to us through the sights and sounds that surround us every day.

God also reveals Himself in specific ways, the most specific today being through His Word, the Bible. Second Timothy 3:16-17 says, "All Scripture is inspired by God and profitable for teaching, for reproof, for correction, for training in righteousness; so that the man of God may be adequate, equipped for every good work." Scripture is inspired, or breathed, by God, so that we may know and act in a way that brings Him honor and glory.

One of the most clear and objective ways God speaks to us today is through the Bible. I believe God speaks through other means beyond the Bible, but we will find the Bible to be the clearest and most easily understood method of our communicating God. Although other means of heavenly communication exist, other than the Bible, it is extremely important that you wrap your mind and your heart around this next thought: God will never contradict Himself. Did you get that? God will never say one thing in the Bible and tell you something else totally opposite through another means. I had a man once tell me it was God's will for him to leave his wife and marry the woman with whom he was having an affair. That's a little odd because the Bible is really clear that God hates divorce (Malachi 2:16), and he would bring judgment upon the adulterer (Ezekiel 16:38). For God to tell this man to leave his wife, God would be lying.

God will not say one thing in the Bible and another thing to our heart. His voice is always in sync with His written Word. As a matter of fact, the Bible should be our measuring stick as to whether or not God is really speaking. If you sense God is prompting your heart with a more subjective means of communication, go back to the Scripture and look for confirmation. His still small voice will always be in agreement with his clear, inspired Word.

The more subjective means whereby God will speak to us can include things such as dreams, friends, feelings in our hearts, and promptings in our minds. I have found that when God speaks to me through one of these more subjective methods, He is usually using the subjective method only as a tool to deliver the objective method, the Bible. I may be concentrating on a particular problem or looking for an answer to a challenging circumstance, and God will remind me of a scripture I have previously memorized or studied. I may be about to make a bad decision about something, and one of my friends will come forward with a biblical principle that gives me clarity on the situation. I might even have a dream, and then while thinking about the source of that dream, God may prompt me with additional biblical insight that suddenly leads me to understand the dream was not just pizza at midnight, but a divine, nocturnal visit.

God does speak, and we are desperate to hear His voice. Paul told us to receive the spoken Word of God, which basically says to me that God is speaking whether we hear Him or not. It is our responsibility to stay tuned in, or we will never be able to discern His voice.

The Role of God's Spoken Word in the Last Days

Think for just a moment how important this weapon of receiving God's Word is to living in the last days. It is possible that God's written Word may become less accessible. I know that is hard to imagine right now, but I had a hard time imagining legalized homosexual marriages ten years ago. If we do not have copies of God's written Word, I think you can see how critical it is that we have hidden God's Word in our hearts and that our hearts are tuned in to God's quiet promptings.

As the return of Christ draws ever closer, I do believe spiritual conflicts will increase. This probability means that Christians must be ready to engage the enemy in the heat of battle. You can imagine how ineffective it would be to face a spiritual conflict and call a time out so we can peruse our concordance in an effort to determine whether or not God has said anything about this particular issue. By the time you stumble across a biblical principle, Satan will have run you through with a fiery arrow. When Satan comes along with temptations, we must have our minds tuned in to the voice of God. This fine-tuning will not happen unless we acknowledge that God speaks and we anticipate hearing His voice.

When I was a little boy, I lived in Augusta, Georgia. One of the wonderful things about our home in Augusta was that we had what seemed like miles and miles of woods behind our home. This environment was a great place for a boy to grow up. My siblings and our friends played in Three-way Creek, swam in the canal leading to the Savannah River, slid around on ice-covered ponds in the middle of nowhere (I don't recommend playing on thin ice, and I'm thankful for a Mama who prayed for her boys), and discovered all manner of mischief in which to be involved.

One day my older brother pointed out the sound of a whip-poor-will. These little birds blend in with their surroundings so well, it is rare to spot one; however, it is not rare to hear one. They make this call that sounds like their name: "whip-poor-will." Here's the interesting thing. I had been in the woods a lot in the early days of my life, but I had not noticed this bird that often. After my brother told me what they were called and pointed out their sound, I was suddenly surrounded by the creatures all the time. So, what happened? Did the birds suddenly appear after I learned about them? Had they been hanging back in the dark recesses of the woods around Three-way Creek waiting on my brother to give me a lesson about the birds? Of course not. The birds had been hiding out in the woods all along, but once I learned about them and became aware of their voices, I tuned in.

God is much the same way. He is speaking and revealing Himself all the time. The question is, "Are we listening?" Are we aware of His soft promptings in our hearts? Are we meditating on His Word to prepare our minds for those promptings in battle? In the last days, many will be confused about truth, and Christians will be tempted in all manner of ways. As we receive the sword of the Spirit, we are constantly turning the dial of our minds to receive God's messages. This sensitivity means that every morning we lie in bed getting our mind focused on the things of God. It means all day long we are disciplining our minds to weed out the distracting thoughts that provide serious competition to the still small voice of God.

Using God's Word as an Offensive Weapon

We must also think of God's spoken Word as an offensive tool. While defense in the spiritual conflict is about protecting our minds and our actions so that the enemy does not gain ground in or through our lives, offense is the process of taking ground that the enemy once held. That means that when a friend is in bondage because of a habitual sin, we use God's Word that is prompted in our hearts or otherwise delivered to our minds to help our friend defeat the enemy. It means that through God's spoken Word, we take our thoughts captive by the truth God is speaking to our hearts, and we defeat the evil one in the heat of battle; otherwise, we will cave in to his menacing deception.

Using God's Word offensively also means that we speak God's truth that has been delivered to us to another heart that has been prepared through God's supernatural work. We pass people every day in whom God has been working. He may be working through difficult circumstances, heartache, or loss, but somehow God has softened up an otherwise hardened heart. If we are tuned in to God's voice, we will hear Him telling us to engage this person with the truth of the gospel. We should have "God at work" antennas up every day as we pass people so that we will be sensitive to the people God is preparing for our ministry.

We can go up and witness to people in general, and we should, but when we are listening to God's promptings, He will send us to people He has prepared for a divine encounter. It was not a coincidence that when Phillip encountered a chariot at the crossroad going from Jerusalem to Africa, the Ethiopian sitting in the chariot was reading from Isaiah. Isn't it amazing that in that story in the eighth chapter of Acts, the man went to church to find God, but left having never found Him? I wonder how many people will go to church this Sunday looking for God, but for one reason or another, they won't find Him. I can promise you God is not the problem. In that desert encounter on the backside of nowhere, God had set the stage to not only change the life of a member of the court of Candace the Queen of Ethiopia, but He also enlisted a new Ethiopian missionary. This court official would take the wonderful message of the gospel back to Ethiopia once again expanding the reach of the church to a new place in the world.

What would have happened if Philip had not been listening when God told him to leave Samaria and go into the desert? If you look at a map, it appears that the way one would travel from Samaria to Egypt is different, in part, from the way people normally traveled from Jerusalem to Egypt. The Jerusalem road joins the Samaritan road, and it was at that exact intersection where Philip met the eunuch. Maybe I'm making a bigger deal out of this encounter than I should, but I don't think so. It seems to me if Philip had hesitated one or two minutes too long, he would have missed his divine appointment. It is a great story of the spoken Word of God making offensive progress through the life and ministry of a willing, listening servant.

The return of Jesus is getting ever closer, and time is running out for people to be saved. We must be sensitive to where God is working so we can make significant Kingdom advances with the wonderful message of the gospel. Such effectiveness calls for a prepared church, but it also calls for a listening church. We should awaken every day with the realization that God has a divine appointment with someone scheduled in our lives, and He is going to use us to make the spiritual connection that could indeed change a life for eternity.

I think that by now you have probably ascertained that we have a part in hearing God's voice. We must regularly be hiding God's Word in our hearts, not only so that we will not sin against God (Psalm 119:11), but also so we will be ready to hear God speak as we engage the enemy. God will many times use His memorized Word to apply His written Word to a unique situation through His spoken Word. This application of the sword of the Spirit is not going to happen unless we are reading and memorizing God's Word, and we are sensitive to His promptings so we will know where to "swing the sword."

Our enemy is swinging his sword, and he is taking out people right and left. People are falling victim to all manner of addictions, abuse, and immorality. It is time for us to swing our sword. The awesome reality is that God's sword is never inferior. As long as we receive His Word and put it to work, we will not be defeated by the enemy. We will stand strong amidst temptation; we will take ground that once belonged to the enemy; and we will have the wonderful privilege of seeing countless people come to faith in Christ.

God is speaking. Can you hear Him? You can if you will tune in and grasp the sword of the Spirit.

CHAPTER ELEVEN

Prayer – The Final Piece

All of this talk about the last days can be depressing, if we don't have the proper perspective. Watching the news at night and seeing various political leaders make poor decisions that will lead into even greater bondage can really send us into a spiral of the doldrums. Years ago, I read the following statistics presented by Dr. Walter Cavert.

Forty percent of the issues we worry about will never happen.

Thirty percent are about the past that can't be changed.

Twelve percent are related to the criticism of others, which is mostly untrue.

Ten percent are about our health, which gets worse with worry.

Only eight percent are about real problems that will be faced.[1]

Mark Twain supported this comment when he said, "I am an old man and I have known a great many troubles, but most of them never happened."[2] Even though we know these facts to be true, worry and anxiety are killers in our American culture today. A recent Washington Post/ABC survey showed that fifty-six percent of Americans worry about what lies ahead for our world.[3] This study reveals the highest percentage of worriers in this particular survey's eleven year history.[4]

One thought that should be considered about some of these issues we have discussed, such as an economic crisis, a one-world government, persecution of Christians, great deception, and the rise of the Antichrist: they will happen. If our choice is worry, we can at least find comfort in the fact we are worrying about something that falls into the eight percent of experiences that we will face, but choosing to worry presents several problems. First, worry does not fix the problem; it only makes our struggles worse. Worrying is also unhealthy, for it creates stress that can lead to all manner of problems. Finally, worry is simply wrong. Philippians 4:6 tells us in no uncertain terms not to worry: "Be anxious for nothing, but in everything by prayer and supplication with thanksgiving let your requests be made known to God." This verse presents to us God's thoughts about anxiety: don't worry about anything and pray about everything.

Fear versus Faith

We worry about paying our bills, resolving our conflicts, and keeping our jobs. We worry about the state of the economy, whether or not we are going to be attacked by terrorists, and the cost of gasoline. While some of the challenges we worry about seem legitimate, others are kind of crazy. With all this worry, we find prayer to be at the bottom of our "to-do list." It is interesting that prayer is our last resort when Philippians 4:7 says when we pray, "The peace of God, which surpasses all comprehension, will guard your hearts and your minds in Christ Jesus." Who wouldn't want the peace of God to guard their hearts and their minds? The times the Bible calls "the last days" will be very conflicted, and we will find real peace only comes in response to our steady faith and persistent prayers. It is because of this truth that Paul ends his discussion on spiritual armor with a call to prayer:

> With all prayer and petition pray at all times in the Spirit, and with this in view, be on the alert with all perseverance and petition for all the saints, and *pray* on my behalf, that utterance may be given to me in the opening of my mouth, to make known with boldness the

> mystery of the gospel, for which I am an ambassador in chains; that in *proclaiming* it I may speak boldly, as I ought to speak (Ephesians 6:18-20).

It seems as if Paul is telling us that while prayer is not actually a piece of the armor, it is the means, or at least part of the means, by which our armor is put into place, and the enemy is engaged.

Prayer is probably a familiar topic to most people. While the word may be familiar, I'm afraid the practice may still be misunderstood. It may not only be misunderstood, but it may also be rarely practiced. I tend to agree with philosophy professor Dallas Willard when he said, "The 'open secret' of many 'Bible believing' churches is that a vanishingly small percentage of those talking about prayer and Bible reading are actually doing what they are talking about."[5]

Prayer can be viewed as a practice or exercise very much like a trip to the grocery store or ten repetitions of sit-ups. Many people participate in prayer at some level, and as Dallas Willard said, "Their track record, as means for actual transformation of individuals into Christ-likeness, is not impressive."[6] In other words, one who prays the Lord's Prayer may be as apt to follow the prayer with a string of obscenities or slanderous comments as easily as placing an offering in a bucket or extending a gentle hand of kindness toward someone in need.

Prayer that Touches Heaven

Basically, it is possible to practice prayer without really praying. By this statement, I mean we can fall into the external appearance of prayer, saying the right words and giving the visual aura of a true supplicant, while never entering the blessed throne room of our Creator. This kind of practice can lead individuals to a human-centered, selfish practice in which the outward expression appears to be authentic supplication while the inner heart is bent on the meaningless repetition that comes from the heart of a modern day Pharisee. Sometimes the one praying has no intention of convincing anyone of their deep spiritual nature; instead, the repetitive exercise has simply become a regular part of their personal culture. For example, some families pray before their meal, and the words spoken become so familiar the whole family could say the prayer in unison. Words are spoken out of the habitual practice, but heaven is not touched by this familiar verbiage.

We readily admit it is possible to pray words and never touch heaven. I can't imagine a Christian really being satisfied with spiritual noise when they could enjoy meaningful conversation. We could easily define prayer as conversation with God, but our definition must go deeper. Although prayer is an act, it is also a life. While it is an experience with God, it is also an expression of God in the deeper recesses of our being. Prayer not only reaches for God, but it also reaches from God. Richard Foster wrote a book on prayer and said, "This book is about a love relationship: an enduring, continuing, growing love relationship with the great God of the universe...Loving is the syntax of prayer."[7] Prayer is the life we live together with Jesus. It is a loving, growing, vibrant relationship with our Creator whereby we continuously connect our heart with His, and His mission becomes our purpose.

While prayer is an extension of and a means to our relationship with God, it is also a practice by which our hearts are molded to embrace the passions of God. Dallas Willard focused on this aspect of prayer, along with other spiritual disciplines, when he said, "A discipline for the spiritual life is, when the dust of history is blown away, nothing but an activity undertaken to bring us into more effective cooperation with Christ and His Kingdom."[8] This concept means that as we grow in our love relationship with Jesus through a life of prayer, our view of the world sharpens with understanding, and our mission in life becomes one with Christ. We have no greater desire than to see His Kingdom advance and the glory of Jesus proclaimed to the world.

Being that the world will get darker with sin as the return of Christ draws ever closer, we need not be too perceptive to understand the necessity of the Christian viewing the world and the Kingdom of God from God's perspective. As the beginning of the Tribulation Period gets nearer, the lines will be drawn more darkly, distinguishing between the Kingdom of Almighty God and the kingdom of the prince of the power of the air. It is through prayer that our hearts are drawn to the heart and purpose of Christ, and we become active participants in the King's army advancing the cause of Christ in these final days before His return.

Praying in the Spirit

Let's return to Ephesians 6:18. Note that God inspired Paul to begin this section with a command: "With all prayer and petition, pray at all times in the Spirit." The obvious command is "pray," but it is interesting to see how he set this teaching up. Do you see the repetition of the word "all?" He is telling us to pray "with all prayer" and "pray at all times." It is as if Paul is saying we should be consumed by prayer. The conjunction, "and," obviously connects this concept of prayer to putting on our spiritual armor. It seems like Paul is assuming we are praying, and he gives us some encouragement and guidance on how to pray. He says we are to "pray in the Spirit." This command is really kind of interesting because a silent inference is made with this statement. If we are told to pray "in the Spirit," this choice of preposition means it is possible for us to pray "out of the Spirit." What does praying in the Spirit or out of the Spirit look like? Can a Christian really pray out of the Spirit? The answer is a resounding yes, but let's consider this concept with some detail.

First of all, praying in the Spirit invites us to a personal relationship with Christ. Paul told the Romans, "However, you are not in the flesh but in the Spirit, if indeed the Spirit of God dwells in you. But if anyone does not have the Spirit of Christ, he does not belong to Him" (Romans 8:9). Praying in the Spirit requires us to have the Spirit, which calls us to a relationship with Jesus. If you are a Christian, the Spirit of God lives in your life. This verse makes it clear that if the Spirit does not live in you, then you are not a Christian. The basis for Paul's mandate to pray in the Spirit is a personal relationship with Jesus Christ.

Praying in the Spirit means more than just being a Christian. Earlier I asked if a Christian could pray "out of the Spirit," and I believe that experience is definitely a possibility. Praying in the Spirit also means praying according to the context of our relationship with Christ. It means praying with the vibrancy and leadership of the Spirit Who now resides in us. It is sort of akin to being filled with the Spirit. It is possible for a Christian not to be filled with the Spirit. I know this reality is so, not only from personal experience, but also from the fact that Ephesians 5:18 commands us to be filled. If being filled were not an option, God never would have commanded Christians to be willing to choose to obey this command to be filled. In addition, the command to "be filled with the Spirit" is a present passive imperative, which means that it is not only a command (imperative), but it is also passive, which means we are acted upon. Think about that truth just a moment. We are commanded to be acted upon. This idea means God is waiting for our permission to consume our being. He does not take charge of every aspect of our lives unless we willingly submit to Him. Also note that the verb is present tense, and present tense signifies continuous action in the Greek language.

This process of submitting every part of our being to the complete control of the Holy Spirit is not a one-time experience. It must be repeated constantly (continuous action). Somewhere in my life, I heard someone say "It's really not an issue of getting more of the Spirit, but rather allowing the Spirit to have more of us." Praying in the Spirit, therefore, is the process of allowing the Spirit of God to direct our prayer life in such a way that our prayers are in step with God's character and cause, but this choice requires daily, or even moment-by-moment, surrender. Seminary professor T. W. Hunt expressed it this way: "Our orientation to everything in life is to be spiritual. If we are filled with the Spirit, the mind and purpose of the Spirit will take precedence over every attitude. The Spirit will govern our thinking, will be the major influence in every decision, and will be observable in all our actions."[9] The effectiveness of your prayer life will come in direct response to the consistency of your journey with Christ.

Praying with All Kinds of Prayer

Do you remember how Paul admonished us to "pray with all prayer?" The New International Version translates this "pray with all kinds of prayer." The idea is that prayer is not limited to only one expression. For most people, prayer means asking God for something. Certainly, God does want us to ask. He actually commands us to do so: "Ask, and it will be given to you; seek, and you will find; knock, and it will be opened to you" (Matthew 7:7). By the way, this passage is a command. God is actually commanding us to ask Him to meet our needs.

Sometimes we feel bad about asking God for anything, but we can find comfort in knowing we are simply obeying His command. I can relate to this idea as a father. I want my children to ask me to help them when they are in need. The only problem I have is that my bank account has limitations. I have great news: God's account is not limited! Granted, He does not always give us everything we want, but He always gives us everything we need. We find that as we "remain in Him" (John 15:5) our requests become increasingly more shaped by His nature and mission and less by our selfish desires. That's why John 15:7 says, "If you abide in Me, and My words abide in you, ask whatever you wish, and it will be done for you."

In days of difficulty and need, God is commanding us to ask of Him. When we face challenges and complexities on the battlefields of life, God wants us to come to Him and ask for wisdom (James 1:5), protection (2 Thessalonians 3:3), provision (Matthew 6:31-32), and boldness (Ephesians 6:19). In future days, we will have experiences where we discover God is our only source of provision and help. I know in the past we have said or sung, "Christ is all I need," but as I once heard someone say, "I'm not sure we can know that Christ is all we need until Christ is all we have." Our resolve will be challenged when we find ourselves being the brunt of government persecution or our resources being completely depleted. Remember the enemy of our soul is working to demoralize us and destroy us, but God says cry out to Him. He says, "Ask, and it shall be given you."

While we probably understand the asking part of prayer from our previous experiences, more aspects of prayer should be considered as we prepare to stand firm in the last days. God commands us to practice intercessory prayer through which we focus our requests on the needs of others (James 5:16). While much could be said about petitions (prayer for ourselves) and intercession (prayer for others), I would like to focus our attention on praying so we can stand firm in the days ahead.

We must pray for boldness for one another as we face inquiries from people who are really seeking answers and from arrogant challenges from others who really want to trip us up. We need to pray for discernment for our children as they are bombarded with greater temptations than previous generations have had to endure. We need to pray for our Christian friends, as well as ourselves, as our enemy seeks to undermine our moral purity, our healthy families, and our sense of mission in a dark world. We must pray for our pastors and our missionaries, our president and our other political leaders, our friends and our fellow church members, and the people within our sphere of influence who desperately need Christ. Intercessory prayer is a significant weapon in our spiritual armory if we are going to make Kingdom advances while the enemy is emboldened by what appears to be a weak church.

Another type of prayer that is critical in spiritual warfare is the prayer of praise. Do you remember in the Old Testament when Moses put the musicians in the front of the battle line (2 Chronicles 20)? Have you ever thought about how crazy that was? Usually musicians are not hardened soldiers. I can imagine a significant difference between a burly soldier and a first tenor. I'm not making a derogatory statement about first tenors because I am one. I'm just saying if I were going into battle, I'm not sure I would want to put the choir out front. While I wouldn't use this tactic, God did.

Praise is a powerful weapon, and worship is an amazing tactic in spiritual warfare. As we sing out our praise to the Lord Almighty, we are declaring that He alone is our victory. It's kind of like what the

Psalmist said in Psalm 20:7, and I especially like how the New International Version translates it, "Some trust in chariots and some in horses, but we trust in the name of the LORD our God." When praise is our priority, we are declaring our trust is in God and God alone! While our enemy seems fearsome and even overwhelming, God is always bigger and stronger. When we declare God's nature with our songs of praise, we are putting everyone on the battlefield in proper perspective. While our enemy seems strong, God is God Almighty. While our enemy seems to be exceptionally knowledgeable, God is omniscient. When Satan seems especially slippery and deceitful, God is truth Who cannot be silenced. While the devil seems to pitch us into the darkest of nights, it is Jesus Christ, the Light of the World, that shines brightly extinguishing the darkness.

Our praise causes us to clearly see our adversary even as we declare God as He really is. Is it any wonder that the hosts of hell flee at the name of Jesus? Should we be surprised when the weakest Christian becomes an immovable saint just at the mention of Jesus, our Leader in Battle? Revelation 17:14 says, "These will wage war against the Lamb, and the Lamb will overcome them, because He is Lord of lords and King of kings." Through worship we are declaring that Jesus Christ is our Leader in Battle because He is indeed Lord of lords and King of kings. In the last days before the return of Christ, we need a worshipping church because a worshipping church is a victorious church.

Should we be surprised that Satan has worked to shut down the church via the "worship wars" throughout history? Battles over worship styles didn't start when the brazen young worship leader sneaked a drum set in the sanctuary behind the organ. All throughout history, Satan has orchestrated infighting over musical tastes because he knows the more we fight each other, the less we praise God together. He wants a weak, divided church, and a church that does not engage in worship is emaciated and debilitated before an intimidating foe. As we consider praying with all kinds of prayers in the last days, we must be sure that we not only know how to praise, but also that we engage in heartfelt worship where the nature and character of God are declared with passion and gratitude from our lips and from our hearts.

While we pray for a revival in the church, let's target our prayers and our efforts toward a revival of real, authentic worship where Jesus Christ is lifted up. Here's the amazing thing: As we lift up Jesus in genuine worship, we too are drawn together. I know that when Jesus said, "And I, if I am lifted up from the earth, will draw all men to Myself" (John 12:32) that He was talking about salvation, but I also believe that when the church lifts up Jesus in worship, the body of Christ gathers together at the foot of the cross in beautiful unity that causes the gates of hell to shake off their hinges.

Another kind of prayer that must come from the lips of last days' saints is the prayer of repentance. I recall a book written in the 70's called *Whatever Became of Sin?*[10] I can tell you what happened to sin. It has been running rampant and loose on planet earth wreaking havoc and destruction. It is destroying lives and families, it is crumbling nations, and it is carving a path of least resistance which leads unsuspecting men, women, and children down a route to destruction. Jesus foretold the nature of our times in Matthew 24:37 when He said: "For the coming of the Son of Man will be just like the days of Noah." Surely part of His comment is pointing to the surprise people will have with their own seemingly sudden destruction, but we can't help but also connect Christ's comment to the sinfulness that typified the times.

I have spoken in previous chapters of other passages of scripture that point to the sinfulness that will engulf us during these final days. I wish I could say these verses related only to nonbelievers, but that is not true. If the church is going to stand in the last days, we must honestly acknowledge our sin before God and seek to walk in personal purity. The problem with an ever increasing immorality is that it is easy for believers to allow the world to become their standard instead of Jesus. We are told to keep our eyes on Jesus, Who is the Author and Finisher of our faith, not the world, which is the destroyer and criticizer of our faith. If the world becomes our standard, we will slip into deeper immorality, and the church will be desensitized to our need for repentance.

Alert Praying

While last days saints must pray with all kinds of prayers, we must also pray with an ever-growing alertness. After admonishing us to "pray in the Spirit," Paul concludes Ephesians 6:18 with the command to attentiveness: "With this in view, be on the alert with all perseverance and petition for all the saints."

The word "alert" comes from a compound Greek word which means "to hunt" and "sleep." Vincent said, "The picture is of one *in pursuit of sleep*, and therefore *wakeful, restless*."[11] I think the point is that we are living in a time when we could easily be lulled to sleep, as the prophetic clock is getting close to the strike of midnight, but we must stay solidly awake. I liken this concept to trying to drive somewhere late at night while fighting sleep. I think God is saying, "Do not go to sleep! Stay awake and pray." It is like what He told His disciples in the Garden of Gethsemane (Luke 22:45-46): "Why are you sleeping? Get up and pray that you may not enter into temptation."

While God calls us to readiness, what are the things about which we should be alert? We must be alert to the times. Peter told the early church, "The end of all things is near; therefore, be of sound judgment and sober *spirit* for the purpose of prayer" (1 Peter 4:7). Satan would like nothing more than to hit the church with a sneak attack, but God commands the church to be watchful and aware. It is kind of like the old "frog in the kettle" illustration where the frog does not jump out of the pot of water on the stove because the water is heated up gradually, so the frog is unaware of the temperature change.

If we are not aware of what is going on around us, we are not aware that Satan has turned up the heat in the spiritual battle. As I wrote about previously, Jesus gave us some of the signs of His return in Matthew twenty-four, and in verse forty-two, He specifically commanded us to "be on the alert." He wants us to be cognizant of the signs as they happen so we will not be caught by surprise. This idea made me think of the sons of Issachar who in 1 Chronicles 12:32 are described as "men who understood the times and knew what Israel should do." We must be just like them so we will know what to do. If we are not alert, we could get discouraged or defeated. If we see events happening around us and connect them to end-time prophecy, we will be more likely to engage the enemy through the power of Christ and realize His return is soon.

We must also be alert to the activity of God. Jesus said, "My Father is working until now, and I Myself am working" (John 5:17). As the night gets darker, we may be tempted to wonder if God is still around. God is at work. Sometimes His work is obvious and always before us, while other times His work may be more subtle. It is important for us to remind ourselves that when God is working quietly, He is still working. I think we must be aware of God's work so we will not "grow weary and lose heart" (Hebrews 12:3).

As Satan's activity grows during these times, it would be easy for us to become discouraged. A time is coming when the church in America will be persecuted. I think you can readily see how we will be tempted to feel that God has abandoned us. I wonder if the first century church in Rome felt abandoned by God during Nero's unbelievable persecution. We must remind ourselves often that God is at work. This reminder will bring courage, boldness, and faith. It will encourage the down-hearted and embolden the church.

Another reason we must be alert to God's activity is, as Henry Blackaby said, "God's activity is an invitation for us to join Him."[12] God is at work in our world, and if we want to be in on what God is doing, we must join Him in His work. One sign of the self-centered church of our day is that we typically ask God to bless what we are doing instead of doing what He is blessing. This concept is missed because it requires our focus not to be on what we can do for God, but rather on what God is currently doing in the world. We can experience a hypnotic satisfaction by thinking about what we can do for God. It makes us feel sort of like a super hero or the Lone Ranger, and we think we are able to reach deep into our lives and abilities and overcome the enemy around us.

The problem is that we do not have anything to bring to the table when it comes to spiritual warfare. Our sufficiency is in Christ, and any spiritual success we have is only because He is at work in and through us. It is critical that we remind ourselves that the only good in us is God in us. If we are going to be a part of the Kingdom advances in the last days, we must be sensitive to where God is working. We must listen and look for "signs of the battle" and then join God's regiment so we can experience His power working through us to defeat the enemy. This kind of perception means that as we talk with our friends and even people we do not know, we are listening for evidence that God is at work in their lives.

I recently had an experience that reminds me of this truth. A while back, I gave an unbelieving young friend a copy of *Case for Christ* by Lee Strobel. A young lady works in a store I frequent, and whenever I'm in the store, I try to engage her in conversations that may give me opportunity to share Christ. When she told me she was looking into various religions, I asked her if she had considered Christianity. The following week was her twenty-first birthday, so I gave her Strobel's book as a gift. Now, fast forward about six or eight months. I was back in the store and talking to another employee. Out of the blue she brought up the book I had given to the other young lady and mentioned that her fellow employee was supposed to let her borrow it, but she hadn't done so yet. It was like God was saying to me, "Hello Private Riordan. Welcome to the front lines."

I can be pretty dense, but in that moment of clarity, I realized that if I wanted to join God where He was working, I must do something to continue this conversation about the authenticity of Christ's claim. I purchased another copy of the book and gave it to my second friend, and since then, she has opened up about her interest in Christianity.

We can either sit on the side lines or battle on the front lines. Where we station ourselves is going to have a lot to do with how sensitive we are to God's activity.

Not only must we be alert to God's activity, but we must also be alert to Satan's activity as well. Peter said, "Be of sober spirit, be on the alert. Your adversary, the devil, prowls around like a roaring lion, seeking someone to devour. But resist him, firm in your faith" (1 Peter 5:8-9). Earlier in our theme passage, we saw that we are to put on the full armor of God "so that you will be able to stand firm against the schemes of the devil" (Ephesians 6:11). The Greek word for "schemes" is "methodia," and it can be translated as cunning arts, deceit, trickery, and so forth. Kenneth Wuest calls it "a deliberate planning or system."[13] It is easy to see from the transliteration that we get our English word "method" from this Greek word. Satan is very cunning and methodical as he works his plan to kill, steal, and destroy. He wants to hinder the church of Jesus and render us harmless in his attempt to deceive the world. If we are alert to his tactics, we can see them for what they are and not be pulled in by his trickery. I've often thought of Satan's schemes to be similar to the schemes of people creating television commercials. Have you ever noticed that commercials often times sell products through deception? Have you ever noticed that beer commercials always use beautiful, fit women as if to subtly say that beer will make you beautiful and trim? The commercial fails to point out that a can of beer typically contains a little over 150 calories, which is somewhere around 10% of what a woman needs for her daily intake. There is a reason why we sometimes refer to someone's large belly as being a "beer gut."

Come to think of it, television always uses beautiful people to advertise everything leaving us to think that a particular product is going to somehow magically change our lives. We should probably shout out every time some commercial gives us false advertising, "That's a lie." Satan uses the same tactics. If we're not alert, we can be sucked into a lie and fall prey to the enemy's deception. It is through prayer that our sensitivity to God's truth and to Satan's work increases. If we are praying regularly, gaining God's wisdom, we will be more likely to recognize Satan's twisted ways and be able to shout back to him, "That's a lie."

Prayer is critical in our spiritual battle. As truth is twisted, sin grows, the gospel is attacked, and the church is weakened, we must battle the enemy on our knees. We put on our armor every day as we pray through each piece mentally and spiritually, securing it into place. Through prayer we are surrounding ourselves with a spiritual force field that can render Satan and his servants powerless before Almighty God, who empowers us. C.S. Lewis emphasized the importance of prayer in his *Screwtape Letters*. Screwtape, the mentor demon, sends his demonic assistant Wormwood a note of warning: "Interfere at any price and in any fashion when people start to pray, for real prayer is lethal to our cause."

CHAPTER TWELVE

Putting On the Armor

While the battlefields of our childhood games may have been the backyard and the battlefields of nations have been the fields and forests of home and foreign lands, our spiritual battlefields are quite different. As we look at preparing ourselves for spiritual conflict, we must take a few minutes to seek a deeper understanding of the battlefield. It is interesting to think that strategy changes in military conquests depending upon the lay of the land. When I grew up, the plastic army men I played with were painted with dark green colors. While camouflage, in my mind, was supposed to be made up of various shades of green, little boys playing with plastic army people today will notice the colors changed. Because of our conflict in Iraq and Afghanistan, the colors of our soldier's uniforms are now made up of the dessert colors of browns and tans. What's the deal? The deal is that a smart army knows it must adjust to the particular battlefield. If you're fighting in the snow, you wear white. If you're fighting in the dessert, you wear tan. If we do not understand our spiritual battlefields, we will not be adequately prepared for this conflict.

The First Battlefield

The first place the battle begins will be consistent across the board for every Christian. The battlefield of which I am speaking is the battlefield of the mind. When God said in Ephesians 6:10, "Be strong in the Lord and in the strength of His might," He was first referring to the way we think. If we are spiritually flabby in our thinking, we will never have spiritual victory. I am not exaggerating when I say that every spiritual battle begins in our thinking. In a way, we might be able to compare the modern-day soldier by saying our military personnel must be mentally sharp and alert, but I do not think that comparison is adequate. Today's military needs to be sharp in their minds so they can be effective on the battlefield, but it is critical Christian soldiers understand that they must be sharp because the mind *is* the battlefield.

As the reign of King David was coming to a close, and Solomon was about to become king, David challenged his son with these words: "As for you, my son Solomon, know the God of your father, and serve Him with a whole heart and a willing mind; for the LORD searches all hearts, and understands every intent of the thoughts. If you seek Him, He will let you find Him; but if you forsake Him, He will reject you forever" (1 Chronicles 28:9). These were not only wise words for a new king, but they are also important words for a spiritual soldier. We must serve God with our whole heart and a willing mind.

The preparation for battle in our minds begins with making a conscious choice to serve God with our whole being and to offer Him a mind that is willing to be trained and surrendered to His authority. We can look at David's life and see he learned the importance of this truth by experience. At times, he did serve God with his whole heart. Although he was called "a man after God's own heart," there were other times his mind was not so willing to follow the Lord. We learn that this choice is not a one-time experience, and choosing to have a willing mind is very much a part of the battle.

Paul addressed the church at Rome with a challenge to surrender their minds to the Lord: "And do not be conformed to this world, but be transformed by the renewing of your mind, so that you may prove what the will of God is, that which is good and acceptable and perfect" (Romans 12:2). It is so easy for us to take the shape of the world around us, very much like Jell-O might conform to its container. The world is in the process of decay, and what was once repulsive to the average citizen has now become acceptable. Just because something is acceptable in the eyes of our society does not mean it is acceptable in the eyes of God.

If we become spiritually obtuse in our minds, we will find it easy to begin to think just like the world. This type of thinking will lead to sin and disobedience, and before long, we will find that we are not serving God "with a whole heart and a willing mind." This passage in Romans also tells us that when we work at being transformed by renewing our minds, we will know the will of God. With this challenge in mind, it makes a lot of sense why Satan will attack our mental process. If he can get us to conform to the world in our thinking, before long we will not be discerning of the will of God. This spiritual slip will lead to sin and a cold and nonresponsive heart to the things of God. Not only will we fail spiritually, but we will also become ineffective in the task of pointing others to Jesus. Because our minds can provide a means for a frontal attack resulting in spiritual casualties, it is important we pray the prayer of the Psalmist: "Examine me, O LORD, and try me; test my mind and my heart" (Psalm 26:2).

The Battlefield of our Relationships

Another battlefield is our relationships. I do not mean to imply that all of our relationships are conflicted, but I am saying other people in our lives provide our enemy a great resource for tripping us up in our spirit. I want to be careful here and not insinuate that our close relations are our enemies. While your spouse or your children are not your enemy, the enemy might use family conflict to lead you down a path away from God. When a relationship is not running on all cylinders, whether it is a marriage or some other friendship, Satan will engage you through that relational circumstance. For example, consider the words of 1 Peter 3:7: "You husbands in the same way, live with *your wives* in an understanding way, as with someone weaker, since she is a woman; and show her honor as a fellow heir of the grace of life, so that your prayers will not be hindered."

Do not let the fact Peter referred to the woman as being "weaker" cause you to struggle with this passage. I once heard someone compare this word to fine china. Maybe men are like wooden bowls, and women are like a piece of Waterford china, delicate and priceless. Look at the last phrase of this passage. It says that married couples should work on their marriage so that their "prayers will not be hindered." Because we are relational beings, we are greatly affected by the people in our lives. We must realize how important it is for us to nurture our relationships so we relate to one another with honesty and clarity. Satan loves to stir up confusion through poor communication, and he strives to create misunderstandings through erroneous perceptions. With this fact in mind, we must proactively work on our relationships so they become immune to Satan's infiltrating efforts.

Jesus said in John 13:34-35 that everyone will know we are disciples of Christ by the way we love one another. In Christ's prayer, recorded in John 17, He also indicated that the world will know He is the Messiah by the way we relate to one another. It is easy to see why God told us to be "diligent to preserve the unity of the Spirit in the bond of peace" (Ephesians 4:3). When we recognize the battlefield has moved from our minds to our relationships, we will be more prepared to respond to our friends and loved ones with understanding and grace. We will be reminded to handle carefully the words of a close friend when we realize Satan might be using those words to strike us down. Jesus showed that he understood the spiritual warfare that can surface through relationships in Matthew 16:23 when he confronted Peter about his brashness: "Get behind Me, Satan! You are a stumbling block to Me; for you are not setting your mind on God's interests, but man's."

The Battlefield of the World

We must also acknowledge the most obvious battlefield: the world around us. Satan attacks us when we least expect and when we are most likely to be weakened by our friends or our circumstances. We will find that if our minds and our relationships are strong, the physical battlefield of time, place or circumstances, is weakened. For example, if our minds are daily surrendered to God and our marriages are strong in Christ, we are a much harder target for Satan's temptation toward immorality. If we are surrendered to the will of God and mentally understand His sovereign rule over our lives, we will not be adversely affected by the loss of a job or some other financial setback. While Satan will work to use many obstacles in an effort to cause us to weaken in our spiritual resolve, it is our steady faith in Christ and commitment to follow Him regardless of our circumstances that makes the other battlefields of life ineffective in our enemy's hands.

Understanding our battlefields is very important, but if we do not regularly get dressed for battle, we will lose critical spiritual ground. Remember the words of Ephesians 6:10-11: "Finally, be strong in the Lord and in the strength of His might. Put on the full armor of God, so that you will be able to stand firm against the schemes of the devil." Putting something on is as familiar to us as getting dressed for work or school in the morning. While you probably had a variety of options for clothing today, you eventually picked out something and put it on. It required a conscious choice and a little knowledge in how to get dressed. We now get dressed without a thought, but at one point in our lives, getting dressed for the day required serious concentration and help. I don't remember being unable to button my shirt, but I'm sure the exercise was once cumbersome. Putting on spiritual armor can be just like that. While it is something that is learned and may require guidance at first, we must all work to master it if we're going to win the daily battles.

Note also that God tells us to "put on the full armor of God." I mentioned in a previous chapter how critical it is that we not forget a single piece of our essential armament. It is true that we will be better at putting on some pieces of armor than other pieces. For example, you may be really good at arming yourself with the truth of God, but you may not be so good at discerning the voice of God. While God's truth is essential, so is His voice. We need to approach each piece of armor as a spiritual lifeline, and we must discipline ourselves to practice putting each piece in place daily. I suggest we all develop the spiritual discipline of mentally putting our armor in place before getting out of bed.

We should also realize that just because we go through the mental and spiritual exercise of making sure each piece is in place before getting out of bed, this exercise does not mean everything will stay in place throughout our day. You can imagine how easily a soldier's armor could get out of place in the early stages of battle. A helmet could get twisted, a shield could get dropped, or a sword could even get broken. You may have everything in place until you encounter your teenaged son at breakfast. A silly disagreement may be followed with strong words and flashes of anger. You head off to work not realizing you have somehow stepped out of your shoes that were fitted with the gospel of peace. Suffice it to say that we must not just put on all the armor of God; we must *keep* on all the armor of God throughout our day.

Putting on the Belt of Truth

Putting on the belt of truth is not just something that can be done in the bed before we begin our day. We need a resolve in our hearts to accept God's truth and apply it to our lives, but this resolve means very little if we do not know the truth of God. While we can surely see that all of this armor overlaps, it should be easy to note how critical it is that God's truth be regularly tucked away inside of our minds. It is difficult to have faith, to know peace, or to hear God speak if we are not consistent students of the Bible. We must embrace several points of application if our belt of truth is going to be in place.

- Are you regularly reading and studying the Word of God? This is such a critical question, and we find that many Christians do not practice this elemental discipline on a regular basis. God's Word is our spiritual food, and without it, we will spiritually starve to death. Is it any wonder that so many Christians are falling prey to all manner of false teaching? Regular reading and study is not a call to create a spiritual checklist so we can just say we read our Bible today. It is a call to encounter the living God through the pages of His written Word on a regular and consistent basis. Notice that I did not just say read the Bible; I also said we are to study God's Word.

If we are really going to be equipped to recognize false teaching in the last days, we must thoroughly know the truth. Many false teachers will attach their twisted doctrine to enough Scripture so that it is received by those who do not know the Bible. This reality is one reason why being a part of a Bible-believing, Bible-teaching church is so important. One great value of sitting under gifted teachers who are not hesitant to teach exactly what God says, regardless of whether or not the teaching is accepted by our society, is that we are regularly challenged to dig deeper into the Scripture. Being active in a strong, Bible-teaching small group is also important as the truth of God can be openly discussed and studied in the circle of close friendship.

- Are you memorizing God's Word? Many of us have a tendency to think that Bible memory is only for children. Somehow we have even convinced ourselves that because we do not remember things as well now as we did when we were children, we have been given a pass by God on this critical spiritual discipline. Can we all just acknowledge this lie is from the enemy? It is true that our memories are not as sharp as we age, but it just means that we need to develop systems for review. Whenever the Psalmist said, "Your word I have treasured (or hidden) in my heart that I may not sin against You," he was not just speaking to school children. This principle applies across the board. Think about this fact: you memorize important numbers, regardless of your age. If you can't remember certain things, you develop systems that will help you to recall them.

- Are you reading other material that leads you to think about biblical teaching as it relates to other beliefs in our society? I am afraid that Christians have become mentally flabby. We are more familiar with sit-coms and reality T.V. than we are with the philosophies and beliefs that maintain a strong republic. We would rather talk about our favorite sports team than about theological concepts that may strain our brains a little. The Pew Research Center reported that sixty-seven percent of Americans read at least one book in 2012.[1] I have noticed, however, that while people may be reading books, their ability to concentrate on heavier topics is somewhat limited. Marketing strategist Brooks Richey challenged readers to get off the mental junk food diet. He wrote, "Faced with a wealth of media options and little diet will power, we gorge on tasty fast-food entertainment opinion and news media exponentially over substantive content. Bloated with "fatty" and "junk" data, our minds are becoming intellectually distorted."[2]

This intellectual deficiency is leading Christians to lose the ability to engage people in our culture in conversations about critical topics. Many Christians will find it difficult, if not impossible, to defend their faith even though God specifically told us to be "ready to make a defense to everyone who asks you to give an account for the hope that is in you" (1 Peter 3:15). Youth culture specialist Brian Housman underscored our problem well: "Most Christians are completely unprepared to provide logical, coherent, well-examined reasons for their belief in Christianity."[3] Part of the problem is that we would rather read the latest best-selling novel instead of C. S. Lewis. We would rather converse about the upcoming NFL draft instead of talk about the sufficiency of God's grace and our longing for transcendence in our walk with Christ.

- Do you freely talk about truth with other people? Part of wearing the belt of truth involves actively engaging people with the truth in hopes of leading them to faith in Christ. While this concept will come up over and over as we talk about putting on the spiritual armor, we must grasp the fact that an intellectual war is going on that has spiritual ramifications. Christians must grapple with the mentally challenging topics of our day so as to be prepared to engage thinking people on topics that may be presenting a barrier to faith in Christ. Some of these barriers include concepts such as evolution, the failures of the church (Crusades, immorality in the church, events leading to the Reformation, etc.), denominationalism, historicity of Christ, the issue of suffering and pain, and many other topics.
- Do you have a biblical, systematic theology firmly planted in your heart and in your mind? Just the term "systematic theology" makes some people tremble, feeling as if that concept should be reserved for a crotchety, old theologue tucked away in some dark, dusty corner of a theological library pouring over ancient manuscripts. This opinion is not true! Christians must know what they believe and why. Here is a good definition of systematic theology: "a discipline of Christian theology that attempts to formulate an orderly, rational, and coherent account of the Christian faith and beliefs."[4] I encourage all believers to take the basic topics of faith and settle securely in their minds a biblical basis for that belief. Start with what you believe about God – Father, Son, and Holy Spirit. Then develop a biblical understanding of mankind, salvation, the church, and last things. You can purchase some great resources from authors, such as Norman Geisler,[5] D. Martin-Lloyd Jones,[6] and Millard Erickson[7] that will help you in your study. As with any book, just because an author says something, you should not automatically accept that statement as truth. Always go back to the Scripture to formulate Bible doctrine. These

writers will have their perspectives and understandings, but God is the one who determines truth.

- Do you have a growing library of books that are helping you along in your Christian walk? Every Christian should have a good library of helpful resources, and it should include commentaries, biographies, Bible study guides, and books on Christian discipleship.
- Do you include concepts related to biblical truth in your prayer? Prayer is one way we mentally and spiritually put on spiritual armor. As we are putting on our spiritual armor every day, we do so, in part, by reflecting prayerfully on the importance of truth in our lives. Through our prayer, we acknowledge that truth is found only in Jesus Christ and is revealed to us through His Word. I encourage you to imagine yourself being wrapped in Jesus and in His written Word. Through prayer, acknowledge your basic beliefs to God and thank Him for His revealed truth. Declare your stance to the Lord on various theological issues each morning before you begin your day.

Putting on the Breastplate of Righteousness

Mentally and spiritually putting on our breastplate of righteousness is a prayerful process whereby we acknowledge before the Lord, with thankfulness, the righteousness we experience through Jesus Christ. We thank God for the forgiveness that is ours through the cross, and we declare "therefore there is now no condemnation for those who are in Christ Jesus" (Romans 8:1). Before we begin our day, we must surrender our minds, our passions, and our actions to the authority of Jesus declaring that we want Him to live out His righteousness in us today.

Starting our day in a spirit of prayer is not the only way we wear this vital piece of armor. Throughout our day we make choices of obedience, and we must remind ourselves periodically that we wear the righteousness of Christ. We must choose to surrender each moment to

Christ, Who resides in us through His Spirit, allowing Him to live out His righteousness through us in that moment of temptation. When we fail, and Satan comes along whispering accusations into our ears, we remind ourselves that we belong to Jesus. We declare that because of the shed blood of Jesus, which has been applied to our lives, and because of His imputed righteousness, we stand before Almighty God clean and righteous. I encourage you to memorize Romans 3:22-24 and be prepared to quote scripture to yourself and to Satan as you declare your righteous standing before God.

- Have you personally trusted Jesus as your Savior thereby receiving His righteousness? In chapter six, I emphasized our righteousness comes only through Jesus Christ. Most people in America today think that we somehow gain a right standing with God through our own acts of goodness, but the Bible is clear that our only righteousness is Christ. If you want to put on the breastplate of righteousness, it begins by repenting of your sin and trusting Jesus Christ as your Savior. If you would like to read more about what it means to be a Christian, turn to the appendix.
- Have you accepted God's forgiveness through Jesus? Some of you may be thinking this second question is a little similar to the first. We may think that people do accept God's forgiveness when they become Christians, but the reality is that some of us have a very difficult time receiving God's forgiveness after we are saved. While we are forgiven for our sin at our salvation, many of us struggle with guilt from past failures rendering us ineffective in the spiritual conflict. The fact is that when Jesus died on the cross, He died for all sin – past, present and future. One of the greatest challenges for us as Christians is the challenge of accepting God's forgiveness or forgiving ourselves. It requires a huge act of faith to receive forgiveness from the God Who is personally offended by the sins of the world. Putting on righteousness means that we do

choose to receive the forgiveness God so graciously offers to us.

- Are you prayerfully reflecting on your righteous standing in Christ and upon your choice to yield to God's power in your life early each day? Putting on the breastplate of righteousness is done partly by mentally and spiritually reflecting daily upon this concept of Christ's righteousness. As we mentally imagine ourselves strapping on a heavy breastplate, we can remind ourselves that this breastplate is righteousness that provides eternal protection from Satan's tactics. Thank God for your justification in Christ (Romans 5:1) and for His power that works so mightily in you.
- Have you established spiritual strength points in your life that will help you choose righteousness? Strength points can be a number of things, such as specific scripture verses dealing with familiar sins, friends who hold us accountable to commitments we've made, and special places that remind us of spiritual commitments we have made in the past. Remember that Jesus used scripture to fight off Satan, and so must we. For example, we could tuck away scriptures like Galatians 2:20 in our minds, so when Satan comes along tempting us, we fall back on this powerful Word from God: "I have been crucified with Christ and I no longer live, but Christ lives in me. The life I now live in the body, I live by faith in the Son of God, Who loved me and gave Himself for me."

We could also memorize the whole sixth chapter of Romans and begin quoting it as temptation falls upon us. By the time we get to verse twenty-three, we will have been renewed with Christ's righteousness and possess a resolve to once again defeat the evil one. Having friends who pray for us and ask us questions about our personal walk with Christ is also helpful. God did not make us to go into battle alone. I mentioned the idea of creating special places. God had Israel create memorable places throughout their history. Do you remember the twelve stones God had Joshua bring out of the middle of the Jordan River (Joshua 4)? These were to be a testimony to the faithfulness of God. We too can use places and "altars" as reminders of commitments we've made.

- Are you helping others to walk in the righteousness of Christ? We are not Lone Rangers in our spiritual journey. We find help, and we help others from the context of Christian community. Part of experiencing community means that we pray for others, and we encourage others in their spiritual conflicts. I challenge everyone to have a small group of Christians with whom they can meet on a regular basis for prayer, encouragement, and accountability. You will find you win a lot more spiritual battles when you know you are not fighting alone.

Putting on the Shoes of the Gospel of Peace

Maintaining spiritual traction in the ongoing conflict is essential for spiritual victory. Knowing the good news that Jesus died for your sins and rose again from the dead is actually not enough to bring peace into your heart. You must personally receive Christ into your life and submit to His lordship over you. As I have stated in other places in this book, it is at this point of salvation that you enter into a wonderful relationship with your Creator and have peace with God. This peace with God is not the only peace you need in the spiritual battle. Satan tries to bring havoc and distractions into our lives that rob us of our peace and effectiveness. People all around us do not even know what this peace means because they have not experienced a personal relationship with Christ.

- Do you have a regular prayer life where burdens are shared with the Lord and spiritual ground is taken in His name? Remember that according to Philippians 4:6-7 it is through prayer that the peace of God will take its place, like a sentry standing guard over your heart and over your mind. We may be in terrific turmoil, but once we find our personal place of prayer and fall on our faces before the Almighty, God's peace begins to settle over us bringing perspective, strength, healing, and hope. As we move into what may be the last days before the return of Christ, we need to be strong prayer warriors defeating the enemy through this critical means of communication with our Heavenly Father. A regular prayer life means that you have a place, a time, and a system whereby you meet with God. A place and a time are self-explanatory. A system can be something as simple as a notebook where you keep a list of things you are praying about. It can be a journal where you write about your prayer burdens and how God is working through your life and your ministry of prayer. You can pray for certain things on certain days (for example: Monday – pastors, Tuesday – co-workers, Wednesday – missionaries, Thursday – political leaders, Friday – neighbors, Saturday – church friends and services, Sunday – small group members). In addition to this seven-day rotation, you can include those things for which you pray every day: your children and spouse, your lost friends who need the Lord, opportunities God may bring across your path, etc.

- Are you prepared to share your faith and this wonderful gospel with someone who is not a Christian? Being ready is a key part of this piece of armor: "feet fitted with the readiness that comes from the gospel of peace." Have a plan by which you can share with someone how they too can find faith in Christ. A number of useful tools are available to help you with this endeavor. It can be as simple as keeping a few copies of the *Four Spiritual Laws* in your purse or pocket. You could memorize the Romans Road to salvation (Romans 3:23, 6:23, 5:8, and 10:9-10) and be prepared to use those scriptures to point someone to Christ. Write out your personal faith story and be able to share it with someone who is open to hearing how God has changed your life. Practice using "The Bridge" illustration (see Appendix I) and be able to write it out at any time on anything as an illustration of how to come to Christ.[8]

- Are you ready to defend your faith with someone who may not believe the Bible or who may be aggressive toward Christianity? We live in a time when many people do not believe the Bible to be God's Word. We can quote scriptures all day trying to help them see their need for Christ, but our point of reference will never be received. Christians must be prepared to begin spiritual conversations from a different starting point. We need to be able to have conversations about topics that may be barriers to faith. With just a little research, we can find that evolution has so many holes in the theory it could not stay afloat in the pool of goo we supposedly crawled out of. A number of useful methods are available to point people to Jesus using logic and philosophy if we will just take time to read up on a few approaches. Read some books on apologetics to sharpen your mind and help you to think in ways that can be a useful tool in sharing God's peace with those who are in spiritual turmoil.
- Are you at peace with others in your life? Christians must not have unresolved anger or harbored animosity toward other people. God is clear that we must always make the effort to resolve our differences with our brothers and our sisters. If the gospel of peace you have does not lead to peace in your relationships with others, your gospel may not be the right one. Jesus said the world will know you are His disciple by the way you love others (John 13:34-35). You can't pick and choose who those "others" are. If the fruit of the Spirit, which starts with love, is not evident in your life, it is possible the Spirit is not there to begin with. Only you and God know the truth of this matter. Ask God for clarity and begin taking steps toward making your relationships right. This experience will involve asking for forgiveness and granting forgiveness to others. Make a list right now of people you must go see in order to start

living out this principle. As we move into the last days, we must be able to stand together as one. Someone else's salvation may depend upon your relationship with another believer in your life.

Picking up the Shield of Faith

How do you pick up a belief, and once we pick it up, is it possible to lay it back down again? Although much has been said about this topic previously, consider this one kernel of truth as you think about the application of this concept. The words "taking up" come from a Greek word that is in a tense we would compare to a past tense. While the Greek aorist tense is not exactly like our past tense, it is similar. I think one truth God wants us to see is that while our faith may not be fully mature and strong, the seed of faith was planted in our hearts when we became a Christian. Because of this implanted seed at salvation, God can say that "without faith it is impossible to please God" (Hebrews 11:6). At salvation, the shield of faith is put in our hands, or better – in our hearts, and God begins our training for a life of spiritual conflict. It may only be a small seed at first, but faith is still present. For us to be effective in the battles ahead, we must grow our faith and learn how to use this shield.

- Has the seed of faith been planted in your heart through salvation? Each piece of armor calls us to confirm our salvation. This step is a not-so-subtle reminder God has given us to say we cannot defeat the enemy unless we belong to Christ. We must remember that different kinds of faith exist. James speaks of a faith that does not save: "What use is it, my brethren, if someone says he has faith but he has no works? Can that faith save him" (James 2:14)? He even points out in verse nineteen that the demons have enough faith to cause them to tremble, but obviously they are not saved. It is critical that we look at our own hearts and lives and make sure that our faith is authentic.

- Do you believe in and act upon God's promises? This practice is where our faith can be nurtured and developed. It would be a good exercise to create a "God's Promises List." As you read through the Bible and come across a promise God has made to you, write it down in a little notebook or in a file on your computer. During your time of prayer, read through your promises from God and determine the kind of actions needed to demonstrate your faith in that truth. Let me caution you to take all of God's Word to heart when you think about His promises. It is easy to make the Bible say something it doesn't really say.

  When I was a teenage paper boy, I was led to believe by some very sincere Christian people that God had given me dominion over the animals. I was told that God promised me that if I had faith, I could command animals to do certain things, and they would have to obey. The key to success had to do with the amount of faith I could muster up. I thought of this conversation I had with my friends as I stood in front of the fenced-in yard on Daniel Street. The little black and white Boston Terriers were usually put up at this time so I could place the newspaper on the front porch. It was essential the two little devils were locked away because in their past lives they had been piranhas.

  I had the thought that it didn't matter that they were vicious because God had given me authority over them. With the faith that could have moved Stone Mountain, I stepped through the gate commanding the little demons to leave me alone; I even commanded the carnivorous creatures to leave me alone in Jesus' name. In just seconds I had one monster clamped on my leg and the other was dangling by his teeth from my upper arm. I quickly learned that maybe dominion over creation didn't necessarily mean I could command God's creatures at my will. I also learned that no matter how much faith I had, if I were stupid enough to step into a yard with two little tormentors whose bark was not nearly as bad as their bite, I was going to bleed.

Believing God does mean securing passages in the Bible that really are directed toward us and holding on to them for dear life. For example, Jesus did tell us, "I will never desert you, nor will I ever forsake you" (Hebrews 13:5). Do you really believe that verse of scripture? Holding up your shield of faith means that even when you feel alone, you believe with everything in you that God has not abandoned you. Faith means that when we find ourselves in desperate need, we remind ourselves that "God will supply all [our] needs according to His riches in glory" (Philippians 4:19). We then cast aside worry in total confidence that God will step in and take care of us.

- Are you strengthening your faith through daily reading of scripture? I know we have already talked about reading the Bible in other areas, but we must be reminded that our faith is strengthened by God's Word. Remember that God says, "Faith comes from hearing, and hearing by the Word of Christ" (Romans 10:17).
- Are you watching events unfolding on the evening news with full confidence that God is working out His plan? It will be easy in the days ahead to allow ourselves to descend into despair as world events appear to go from bad to worse. We cannot allow ourselves to be discouraged. We must believe that God is sovereign and that nothing happens that does not first pass through His hands. We must really believe that "God causes all things to work together for good to those who love God, to those who are called according to His purpose" (Romans 8:28).
- When you are bombarded with satanic attacks, do you rely upon God and His weapons to defeat the enemy? When you are tempted to sin, you can find great strength for your resolve in the words of Scripture. Picking up the shield of faith means,

in part, that we hold forth the Word of God with great trust in its truth and power. It means that we fall on our faces in prayer knowing that great strength comes as we yield to God's power and presence. It means that we flee to the security of the community of God when we find ourselves attacked and weakened. We can only experience this security if we have strong relationships within the Body of Christ, the church, whereby we can pour out our souls finding replenishment when our resources are weakened.

- Are you determined to trust God fully regardless of what happens in the future? I urge you to make this commitment and allow God to strengthen your faith for the days ahead. I do not know when circumstances will deteriorate to this level, but at some point, Christians in the United States will be openly persecuted for their faith. I know it happened at Columbine, but all of America was appalled at that act of unspeakable violence. A day will come when Christians will be weeded out and harmed because they are followers of Christ. It is happening in other places in the world and will one day take place in our own country. If that happens in your lifetime, are you prepared to remain faithful to God regardless of the pressure to recant your faith?

Putting on the Helmet of Salvation

In chapter nine, I spoke of the three tenses of salvation. I have already emphasized several times how essential it is that we have experienced the past tense concept of salvation through repentance and faith in Christ. This past tense secures our salvation and our home in heaven. It means that we are saved from the penalty of sin, which is eternal separation from God. The future tense of our salvation is going to take care of itself (or at least by God) as we are one day delivered from the presence of sin. It is the present tense concept of our salvation that we are told to "work out." Consider the words of Philippians 2:12-13: "So then, my beloved, just as you have always obeyed, not as in my presence only, but now much more in my absence, work out your salvation with fear and trembling; for it is God who is at work in you, both to will and to work for His good pleasure."

Once you become a Christian, the daily process of putting on the helmet of salvation is making plans to walk in daily submission to Christ as you grow in Christlikeness. The theological word is *sanctification* or *holiness*. Look how Paul addressed the church in Romans 6:19: "I am speaking in human terms because of the weakness of your flesh. For just as you presented your members as slaves to impurity and to lawlessness, resulting in further lawlessness, so now present your members as slaves to righteousness, resulting in sanctification."

- Are you carefully studying God's Word in order to know His directives on how you should live? Once again we are back to the importance of reading the Bible. We cannot "work out" our salvation or grow in holiness unless our minds are filled with the Scripture. Through the Bible, we learn how to live and act in a way that pleases God.
- Have you developed a plan to help you make choices that honor God? It is easy for us to pledge our minds to the Lord in the morning before we go to work, but it's another thing to do it once we are attacked at the office by our co-worker, bombarded with titillating advertisements on the Internet, or face once again the unmet expectations because of an insensitive spouse. If we do not have a strong plan to undergird our resolve to honor the Lord, then we are setting ourselves up for spiritual failure. It is easy for us ıo say, "Oh, I would never do that," but be careful. You may be the next one to fall.
- Do you have a plan for personal growth? I have throughout my life developed a concept of an ongoing strategy for growing in Christlikeness. I can't take any credit for this idea, for it was driven into my mind by a godly family while growing up. I remember times sitting around the kitchen table talking about the books we would read and exercises we would do in the

upcoming year that would help us to grow. It did not take much of a leap for me to figure out I should put this idea down on paper. I watched my older brother develop such plans for his personal growth, and I was inspired to do the same.

Every year, I divide my life up into several areas in which I would like to see growth: spiritual, family, financial, leadership, and ministry. I plan ahead the books I will read in each area that will shape my thinking. I look at various scriptures and pull out passages I aspire to memorize over the following months. I look at a calendar and determine the conferences I will attend, the people with whom I will spend time, and the experiences I will undertake so that my objectives in those areas will be accomplished. I wish I really had it all together and always accomplished my goals, but I will tell you that I do a lot better just because I have a plan. If I ever find myself on my face in failure, it is usually because I have put down my plan, and I am not following my strategy. I've found God uses this discipline to keep me on a path where my thoughts, my heart, my relationships, and my actions are shaped in such a way they honor Him.

Holding High the Sword of the Spirit – the Word of God

The most profound discovery I have had in this area involving the sword of the Spirit is the fact that the "word" is not just the written Word but also the spoken Word of God. In order for me to wield this sword, I must first of all settle in my mind that God does still speak today and that my ears must be tuned in to His voice. I'm going to assume you have settled the first part of the equation–that God still speaks–and focus on the second part of developing our ears so that we may be "quick to hear."

- Are you studying and memorizing significant amounts of scripture so as to fill your mind with the thoughts of God? I know I am sounding like a broken record, but Bible intake is so essential to our spiritual victory that it is included in every piece of the armor. While God may speak subjectively in the quiet places of your heart, He is most likely to use the objective, concrete method of bringing His written Word back to your mind. In order to apply this concept now, you must develop and follow a plan for scripture memory. A number of tools are available to help you develop a systematic plan for scripture memory, and which plan you follow does not really matter. The more scripture you memorize, the better. I suggest you memorize scripture with a partner so as to hold one another accountable.

- Do you spend time quietly meditating on the things of God? Meditating is not something reserved for bald-headed, Eastern guys sitting cross-legged on a colorful mat. When the Bible speaks of meditating in the Old Testament, it uses a Hebrew word that was used to describe a cow chewing the cud. I know the thought of a cow chewing, swallowing, spitting up, chewing, swallowing, spitting up, and so forth is not exactly a pleasant thought, but if you connect this picture to the idea of meditating on Scripture, it can be a useful image. I would encourage you to take time in your day to simply think about a particular passage of Scripture. As you "chew" on the Scripture, you can focus on each word and think about its depth of meaning. Allow God's Spirit to help you draw out all of the spiritual nutrients God placed in His inspired Word. You will find that God will speak to you from this process, thereby developing in you a sensitive ear to His voice.
- Do you spend time reflecting on the events of your life and of our world in connection to the Scripture? We live in a day where we do not typically slow down much, and I am the world's worst at going 100 miles per hour, stopping only as my head collides with my pillow. We must learn to develop the discipline of quiet. We typically connect meditating on Scripture to this discipline, but we should also incorporate reflection

on that which is around us. We will find that God speaks through the circumstances of our lives. I encourage believers somehow to work spiritual retreats into their lives as times of calendared quiet. You might take one hour a day, one morning a week, one day a month, and one week a year for this spiritual exercise. That might be a little overwhelming to pull off, but you could do something to plan times of quiet into your life. This time could include reflection, meditation on Scripture, prayer, and so forth, but it will involve quiet before the Lord.

- Do you listen to your Christian friends knowing God could be speaking through them? It is true that God speaks through His church. It could be the pastor's sermon from Sunday or a comment a friend made over lunch, but God can give you clear direction from other people. The key is learning how to be sensitive to God's voice and to recognize it when our ears and hearts vibrate with its sound.

Standing firm in the last days will not be an easy task, but it is an essential undertaking for Christians individually and for the church corporately. We will encounter spiritual warfare in the days ahead as we have never known it, but we will also experience the greatest opportunity for evangelism in the history of Christianity. Will we be ready? If we are going to engage our world with the life-changing message of the gospel, and if we are going to overcome the enemy as evil forces are being built up for Satan's final, wicked surge against Jesus and His celestial army, then we must stand immovable. What do you need to do to put on the spiritual armor of God making it possible for you to stand firm in the last days? Being immovable is really not an option for the church, though experiencing its reality will require a daily choice by her members. When the winds of heresy and deception blow, will you be immovable holding firmly to the Truth of God? Will you be immovable holding tightly to the Family of God? Will you be immovable living in the glory of God?

The only way you or I will be immovable is if we have tapped into the immovable Lord Jesus Christ Who has equipped us with His effective spiritual armor. As the Psalmist says in Psalm 3:3, God will be our glory and our shield: "You, O LORD, are a shield about me, My glory, and the One who lifts my head." God does not just give us spiritual armor; He is our armor. When we embrace our Creator by putting on His armor for our spiritual conflicts, we will find the words of 1 Corinthians 15:58 to be true about our lives and ministries: "Therefore, my beloved brethren, be steadfast, immovable, always abounding in the work of the Lord, knowing that your toil is not in vain in the Lord."

Appendices

APPENDIX I

How to Become a Christian

Ephesians 6:13 should be quite familiar to us at this point: "Therefore, take up the full armor of God, so that you will be able to resist in the evil day, and having done everything, to stand firm." This appendix is provided to address the first steps of doing "everything to stand firm." The first step is the step of faith leading to salvation through Jesus Christ. If asked, many people in the United States would claim to be Christians, but what does it really mean to be a Christian? How does one "cross over" to a life of faith?

We must first understand a few truths. One critical thing we need to know is that God made us for relationships, and the number one relationship He made us for is the relationship with Himself. While God wants a relationship with us, the fact is that deep down in our hearts, we long for a relationship with God. Sometimes we try to fill that longing with all manner of things such as careers, accomplishments, financial success, patriotism, sex, hedonism… The list could go on and on. In all our attempts to fill the void in our lives, we simply come up empty-handed, or maybe I should say

"empty-hearted." Earlier in this book, I referred to Pascal's quote: "There is a God-shaped vacuum in the heart of every man." If we try to fill the void in our lives with anything other than God, the void will remain just that – a void. Our longing, or our hunger, is for God and God alone.

The Bible teaches that every human being is born separated from God because of sin. Romans 3:23 says, "*For all have sinned and fall short of the glory of God.*" A few verses prior to this, the Bible says, "*There is none righteous, not even one*" (Romans 3:10). Our society has tried to hide the reality of sin, but the fact is sin is not only all around us, but it is also all in us. Sin could simply be defined as missing the mark of God's perfection. It is doing, saying, or thinking anything contrary to the ways and will of God. We are all guilty. We can try to redefine the term or compare ourselves to people of lesser morals, but the bottom line is that every human being is born with a nature to do wrong, and we also occasionally, or not so occasionally, chose to sin. One problem we have is that while we are not righteous, God IS righteous and holy. He can have nothing to do with sin, even though He loves the sinner (see Romans 5:8). This creates a great divide between us and God. The natural result of humanity apart from God is death. Romans 6:23 says, "*The wages of sin is death…*" This concept of death is more than just ceasing to have a heartbeat and a brain wave. This "death" means eternal separation from God.

People do try to get to God through all manner of means. Most people think that if they are good enough, God will give them a pass into heaven. It is almost as if there is a large scale in heaven where all of our deeds are weighed. The good deeds are placed on the plate to the right and the bad deeds are placed on the left. If the good deeds outweigh the bad deeds, then we feel as if God is obligated to let us in to His heaven. The Bible says in Isaiah 64:6 "*all our righteous deeds are like a filthy garment,*" and Ephesians 2:8-9 clearly says we are not saved by doing good works: "*For by grace you have been saved through faith; and that not of yourselves, it is the gift of God; not as a result of works, so that no one may boast.*"

While God is compassionate, merciful, and gracious, He is also holy, righteous and just. If God simply gave us a pass and let us into His heaven, He would not be righteous and just. If He just sent us all to hell with no hope for eternal life, He would not be gracious. God's answer, and our solution, is Jesus Christ. God sent His own Son to die for the sins of the world. John 3:16 says, "*For God so loved the world, that He gave His only begotten Son, that whoever believes in Him shall not perish, but have eternal life.*" Jesus paid for our sins with His own life and then rose again from the dead declaring He is indeed God (see Romans 1:4). God has given to us an option: either we pay for our sins through our own eternal death and separation from God, or we allow Christ's death to pay for our sins as we trust Him as our Savior. In essence, Jesus became our bridge to the Father. Through Jesus Christ, and only through Jesus Christ, we can enter into a relationship with our Creator. Jesus said, "*I am the way, and the truth, and the life; no one comes to the Father but through Me.*" Acts 4:12 says of Jesus, "*And there is salvation in no one else; for there is no other name under heaven that has been given among men by which we must be saved.*"

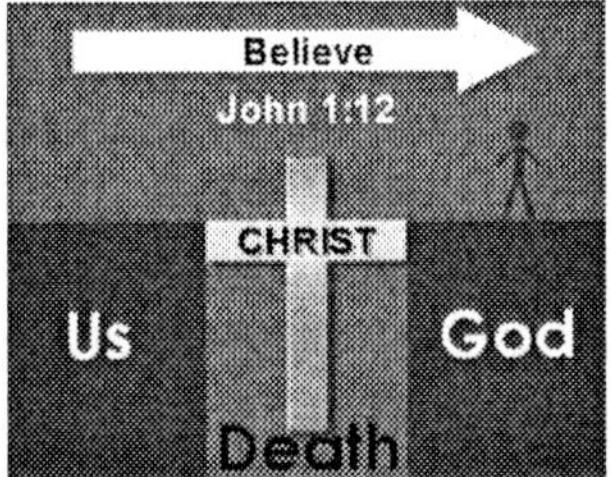

We enter into a relationship with God through repentance of our sin and faith in Jesus Christ. Repentance simply means turning around. Whereas, once we were following our own way and our own desires, to repent means we turn and follow God's way and seek to fulfill His desires. Placing our faith in Jesus means more than just intellectually accepting the facts about Christ's identity and work. The Bible says in James 2:19: "*You believe that there is one God. Good! Even the demons believe that—and shudder*" (NIV). True faith comes as we surrender our lives to Jesus Christ allowing Him to be the King of our heart and the Leader of our life. Romans 10:9-10 says, "*If you*

confess with your mouth Jesus as Lord, and believe in your heart that God raised Him from the dead, you will be saved; for with the heart a person believes, resulting in righteousness, and with the mouth he confesses, resulting in salvation."

Christianity is a choice to surrender to Jesus Christ as the Lord of your life. Surrender means totally giving your life into the hands of someone else. Imagine drowning in a lake somewhere and a lifeguard swims up to rescue you. The only way you can be saved from sure death is to quit fighting and surrender to the saving grasp of the lifeguard. Becoming a Christian is not just praying a prayer. It is not just going to church. It is not just trying to reform your life. Becoming a Christian is turning from sin and self and choosing to follow Jesus as your Sovereign King.

You can express this decision in a prayer as you cry out to God. If you have never done this and would like to, why not bow your head right now and tell Jesus that you acknowledge you are a sinner in need of forgiveness. Tell Him you believe that He died for you and rose again, and ask Him to forgive you for your sin and come into your life. Commit yourself to be a Christ-follower for the rest of your days. Thank Him for His grace and pledge yourself to begin your new life today by seeking to grow as a new believer. I encourage you to do this right now. The Bible says in 2 Corinthians 6:2, "*Behold, now is the acceptable time; behold, now is the day of salvation.*"

What's next? While going to church doesn't save you, it sure helps you grow as a Christian. You will build relationships with other Christians who are seeking to grow in Christ and serve God with their lives. You will be encouraged in your faith and will grow in your understanding of the Bible, God's Word. I encourage you to find a Bible-believing church to attend where the Bible is taught and good Christian friendships can be enjoyed. Is there someone who would like to hear of your decision to become a Christian? Why not call them right now and let them know of your new faith? Do you have a Christian friend whom you admire? Why not call him or her right now and ask if you can go to church with them on Sunday? If you do not have Christian friends with whom you can share your decision, simply tell someone close to you of your decision. If you already attend a Bible-believing, Bible-teaching church, give your pastor a call, and let him know of your decision to trust Christ as your Savior.

Welcome to the Family of God!

Special thanks to Heather Bible Chapel (http://heatherbiblechapel.org) for assistance with "The Bridge" graphics.

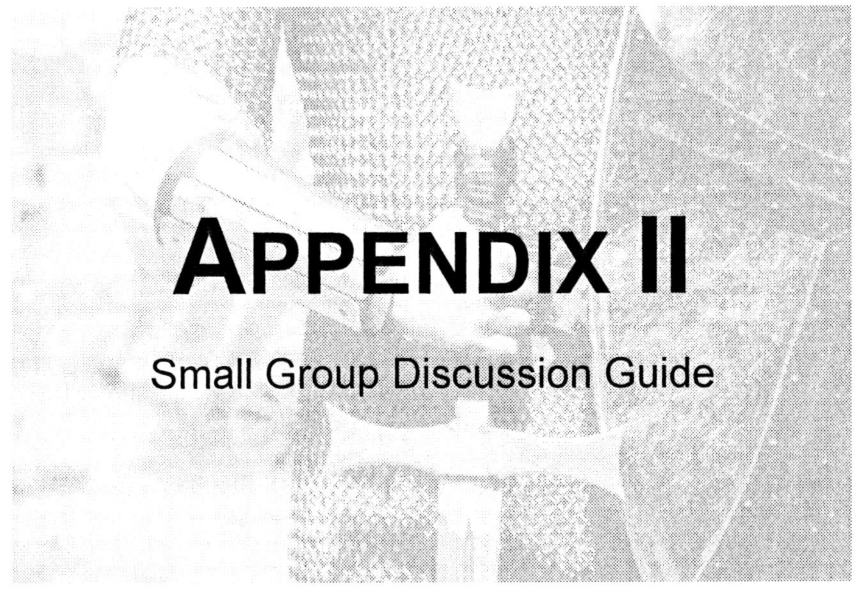

APPENDIX II

Small Group Discussion Guide

Spiritual maturity and meaningful ministry happen best in small groups. This resource is provided for you to help you process the truths of this book with a small group of people who gather for Bible study, prayer, and fellowship. If you do not participate in a regular small group meeting, find a few friends with whom you can discuss these concepts and plan to meet once a week or twice a month. Read the book together, discuss the questions below, determine your personal application on each point, hold one another accountable, and pray for one another.

This discussion guide is divided into six sessions where you will be led to cover two chapters per session. It is suggested that the small group leader begin the session by briefly reviewing the content of the two chapters the session will cover. After the review, the small group leader can guide the group in discussion by using the questions below. You may want to use every question or simply pick the questions that you think will best help your group discuss the topic. May God use your group to be as iron sharpening iron, whereby you will be better equipped to stand firm in the last days.

Session One - Chapters One and Two

1. In response to current events, Tim stated in the opening words of Chapter One that "current events have gotten weird" and "the paradigm of 'normalcy' is shifting." Have you noted that a shift has happened in our world that has created instability? How has this made you feel?
2. Tim asked the question, "What does all this mean?" He mentioned two possibilities that people usually conclude. One is that we are in a "global correction," and these people usually view the future with great optimism. The other possibility is that things on the earth will continue a downward spiral. Christians view this with great anticipation knowing that the rapture is soon coming. What is your view?

Read Matthew 24:1-8

3. The Disciples asked Jesus a question that really contained three parts. What were they? What were the "these things" to which the Disciples referred? You will have to go back and read Matthew 24:2 to answer this question. Did Jesus actually answer all of the questions?
4. Jesus could have used a variety of terms to describe the events leading up to His Second Coming, but He chose the imagery of "*birth pangs*." Why do you think He chose that imagery?

Read Mark 13:32-37

5. Why do you think God has ordained that no one knows when Christ is going to return?
6. Do you see a tension in this passage of Scripture? Jesus first says that no one knows when He is coming again, but then He says, "Watch." What is the significance of this?

7. What are some things you will do at the beginning of this study to "*be on the alert*" for the return of Christ?

Read Matthew 24:4-31

8. Jesus spoke of several signs of His return in this passage of Scripture. Look briefly at the five "signs" Tim described in Chapter Two of this book. Have you seen evidence of these signs being fulfilled in your lifetime?
9. Are we living in the last days? Do the possibilities affect the way you live?

Digging Deeper (additional questions for your consideration):

Read Daniel 2:31-45

1. How would you describe Nebuchadnezzar's dream? What was Daniel's interpretation?
2. Tim said, "We know this is futuristic because there has been no world kingdom since the Roman Empire. It is to be a future Roman Empire with a division of 10 kingdoms or distinct leaders." Do you agree with him? What is the evidence that this empire will be ruling at Christ's Second Coming?
3. Do you believe our world will one-day be ruled by one government? What are your thoughts shared in this chapter pointing to this concept being a strategy of numerous world leaders?
4. Do you think the European Union could eventually become the dominating world power to whom the remaining countries of the world will submit?

Session Two – Chapters Three and Four

1. What comes to your mind when you hear the word "prophecy?" Tim referred to his perception of people teaching on prophecy when he was a boy: "I perceived those speakers to be fortune tellers who would come to town with their charts and illustrations predicting the end of the world." Did you ever share a similar opinion? Have your thoughts about prophecy changed over the years?
2. Tim drew a distinction between physical warfare and spiritual warfare. Paul told us that "the weapons we fight with are not weapons of this world" (2 Corinthians 10:4). What is your response to Paul's indication that we are at war, but we are to fight with supernatural weapons?
3. Tim spoke of the meaning of "be strong in the Lord" (Ephesians 6:10). Discuss the significance of this command to be strong being a present, passive imperative (you may need to go back a read the two paragraphs on pages 33-34).
4. God has given us "armor" to wear in our spiritual conflicts. Discuss the significance of putting on the *full* armor of God.
5. Do you ever get confused about who the enemy is? Have you ever slipped into thinking that people are your enemy instead of Satan? How can you overcome this tendency?

Read 2 Corinthians 11:14

6. Have you ever encountered Satan as "an angel of light?" What was that like? Did you overcome him and his temptation? What is necessary for us to have the victory in these moments?
7. What do you think is the best way to be equipped to recognize Satan's deceptions so you will not fall victim to his schemes?
8. What comes to your mind when you hear the words "spiritual warfare?" Is this a comfortable concept for you?

9. Tim alluded to people's hunger for a vibrant experience with Christ and a growing awareness of spiritual warfare. He said, "Christians in every age group are coming to the conclusion that there is more to Christianity than a sleepy service on Sunday and a lazy attempt to follow the Ten Commandments throughout the week." Does this describe you? Do you feel a "dissatisfaction…with the 'business as usual Christianity' that is void of the supernatural?"
10. In the section entitled "Potential Pitfalls," Tim addressed six potential problems or dangers that can cause Christians to trip up in the desire to understand spiritual warfare. Review these six dangers with your group and discuss whether or not you see these dangers being an issue in people's lives.
11. Tim mentioned three enemies: the world, the flesh, and the devil. Of these enemies, which one receives the greatest attention? Is there a danger that comes from focusing on one enemy and ignoring the other two?

Digging Deeper

1. Tim referred to some things included in Bill Gillham's book *Lifetime Guarantee:* "With that said, Bill Gillham pointed out that while we are made into a new spirit-creation, we have paths already created in our minds and lives that become avenues for the power of sin to bring destruction." What are some examples of these paths? Have you ever known someone (or experienced it yourself) who seemed to overcome an addiction only to fall back into it months or even years later? How can that happen? Is it possible that when we sin, we create paths in our lives making it easier for us to fall in the same way in the future?

Read 1 Peter 5:8-9

2. God tells us to be "alert and of sober mind." What does this mean? How are we to apply this command?
3. What does it mean to compare Satan to a roaring lion? How does this make you feel? What will you do in response to this imagery that shows Satan as being on the prowl seeking to destroy lives – including yours?
4. Tim said, "It is critical that we remember the devil was defeated at the cross, and his defeat was underscored with the empty tomb! Satan is a defeated foe, so we must not allow him to act like the victor in our lives." How do people live as if Satan is not defeated? What difference will it make in your life to refuse to allow Satan to act like the victor in your life?

Session Three – Chapters Five and Six

Read Ephesians 6:10-18

1. Have you considered the meaning of the "spiritual armor" in the past? What do you think about connecting these concepts to equipping believers to stand firm in the last days?
2. What do you think God meant when He commanded us to "stand firm?"

Read 2 Timothy 4:1-5

3. In this passage, God tells us, "For the time will come when they will not endure sound doctrine." Do you think this "time" has come? Do you know of any examples of people not enduring sound doctrine?
4. Do you believe in absolute truth? What is the problem with thinking that truth is relative?
5. Do you agree with Tim's assertion that the United States was founded upon the belief of absolute truth? Why or why not? Does the rise in the belief that truth is relative threaten our country and our churches?
6. Tim quoted Nancy Pearcey: "Training young people to develop a Christian mind is no longer an option; it is part of their necessary survival equipment." How do you think we are to train young people to develop a Christian mind?
7. As we seek to be a "herald of truth," is it possible for us to speak the Word of God without grace? What does that look like? What would it look like to live out the Word of God without grace?
8. Tim said, "What the world so desperately needs to see in these times are Christians who live the Word of God." How might your life change if you really lived out the Word of God?

Read Ephesians 6:10-13, 14

9. In the early words of chapter six, Tim stated, "Regardless of when the rapture happens, a steady decline morally, economically, and spiritually will take place as the stage is set for the final showdown between good and evil." In what ways have you noticed this decline already happening during your lifetime?
10. Tim pointed out that unrighteousness will be the new normal as the world moves toward global unification. What role will putting on righteousness play in the life of believers during this time of moral turbulence? Why do you think God referred to righteousness as a breastplate?
11. Summarize the difference between imputed righteousness and imparted righteousness. How does it make you feel to think that God chooses to place His righteousness upon those who believe in Him? How does this truth affect your motivation for choosing to be obedient and pursue righteous living?
12. Do you see the gradual desensitization toward sin in America? How should believers fight this tendency while remaining gracious and compassionate toward those who are sinning?
13. Tim said this about becoming a Christian: "You are not just praying a prayer, being dunked in water, or attending church services. You are becoming a follower of Jesus Christ. You are signing the title of ownership of your life over to Jesus Christ and placing a sign in your front window that reads 'Under New Management.'" How have you experienced the reality of "new management" in your own Christian experience?

Digging Deeper:

Read 2 Timothy 2:15

1. What does it mean to "do your best to present yourself to God as one approved?" How do we, "correctly handle the Word of God?"
2. Have you ever considered Jesus as being Truth? What does this mean to you?
3. How do we receive the Word of God as the standard of truth? How will we interpret various philosophies and world events if we take this position?

Read Colossians 4:4-6

4. What does it mean to be "wise in the way we act toward outsiders?" How do we let our conversation always be "full of grace, seasoned with salt?" How does the last phrase fit in with the first two admonitions: "so that you may know how to answer everyone."

5. How can wearing the breastplate of righteousness be offensive and not just defensive?

Session Four – Chapters Seven and Eight

Read Ephesians 6:10-13, 14-15

1. Chapter Seven begins with an emphasis on preparation. Tim stated, "If you think about it, being able to stand firm requires preparation, and without this preparation, we will certainly fail. The whole idea of a challenge to stand firm indicates the converse is also true. While we can, and hopefully will, stand firm, it is also possible that we will not stand firm. If you are not standing firm in the last days, you will fall or fail." What do you think success and failure mean in this context?
2. Since God made the words "stand firm" an imperative, we must therefore be responsible for our success on the spiritual battle-fields of our lives. Does this seem a bit unfair to you? If we are under a significant attack from the enemy and fall, can't we blame the enemy? Why or why not?
3. What is your reaction to the idea that thirty percent of the Bible is prophecy? Do you agree that if the Bible is wrong in one area, the whole Bible is suspect? What are some of the prophecies of the Bible that have been fulfilled?

Read 1 Peter 3:15

4. What is your reaction to the admonition that we have an obligation to the world?
5. How does a Christian become ready to give an answer to anyone who "asks you to give the reason for the hope that you have?" Why do you think God included that we should do so with "gentleness and respect?"
6. Go back and re-read the quote from Cornelius Plantinga on page 91. Have you ever felt like you were missing shalom? What caused this to happen? Was this peace ever restored?

7. Tim wrote about three types of peace: peace with God, peace with ourselves, and peace with others. Which one of these is the most challenging for you?
8. Read Philippians 4:4-7 and discuss what it means for God's peace to stand guard over your hearts and minds. How will you apply this verse the next time you have a problem?

Read Ephesians 6:10-13, 16

9. In Chapter Eight, Tim wrote about spiritual conflict and said, "With all this interest in protection, it is amazing to me that we may be least protected in the area that causes the greatest threat." Do you think that Christians are aware of the serious threat by our spiritual enemy? Are you?
10. Do you sense an evil force that is growing in our country today? How about in our world? What are some examples of growing evil in our world?
11. Tim partially defined faith by saying, "Faith means we believe God regardless of the circumstances. It means whether we understand what's going on or we don't have a clue, we still hold on to God and know that He is somehow working His plan." How hard is it for you to hold onto God when problems develop in your life? Have you ever known people to give up on God when they experienced difficulty in their lives?
12. How is the shield of faith a verb instead of a noun?

Digging Deeper:

1. Tim wrote about some of the lies that Satan whispers into our minds. What are some lies Satan has tried to get you to believe?
2. Would you agree that your mind is a battlefield? What role does faith play as you engage in a mental battle with Satan?

3. As times get more difficult, many people will begin to lose faith. How can trusting in God's sovereignty help Christians stand firm in the last days?
4. Can you imagine Christians being physically persecuted in the United States? How will faith help believers endure persecution?

Read Ephesians 6:12

5. What do you think Paul meant when he said our struggle is against "the rulers, against the powers, against the world forces of this darkness?"
6. Discuss with your group a time when you experienced Satan's assault as a "flaming arrow." Do you think the idea of a "slow burn" is a correct description of how Satan sometimes works? What are examples of "secondary blasts" in Satan's attack on people today?
7. What part does faith play when Satan comes at you as a roaring lion?

Session Five – Chapters Nine and Ten

1. Ephesians 6:17 says, "And take the helmet of salvation…" Why do you think God led Paul to compare salvation to a soldier's helmet?
2. Tim said, "It would be easy to see this piece of armor as simply a reminder of how important it is for everyone to become a Christian, but I think the helmet of salvation points to more than just people repenting of their sins and trusting Jesus as Savior." He stressed that salvation has three different expressions, or tenses. The first is the past tense of salvation, or being saved from the penalty of sin. Take a few moments and have a few group members briefly tell their testimony of when they became a Christian and were saved from sin's penalty.
3. Has anyone in the group ever been hit by Satan's weapon of doubt? How did you overcome this onslaught? How might Christians in the future overcome Satan when he plants seeds of doubt regarding their salvation?
4. Because Satan is a deceiver, it is possible for him to deceive people into thinking they are Christians when they are really lost. Tim said, "Praying a prayer does not make someone a Christian. You can say words all day long with the only result being a hoarse voice and a sore throat. Please understand this truth: the real evidence of an authentic faith is a changed life! Hell will be filled with people who lived right, prayed a prayer, and even went to church." Is there anyone in the group who fell victim to being deceived into thinking you were a Christian when in fact, you needed to be saved? How did God open your eyes to your real need for salvation?
5. What does present tense salvation mean? Can anyone give a testimony of recently being saved from the power of sin in your life?
6. How might the promise of God's completion of your salvation give you hope and encouragement during the last days?

7. Ephesians 6:17 says that we are not only to *take* the helmet of salvation, but also the sword of the Spirit. Tim pointed out that the Greek word actually means *receive* as God first takes the initiative to offer His Word to us. What are the implications of this as it relates to God's Word?
8. Tim said, "A first century soldier had the mentality of 'kill or be killed.' We must have similar thinking every day as we step on the battlefield of life. Satan doesn't play, and nor should we." Do you think many Christians are "playing" today and not taking the spiritual warfare seriously? What is the evidence of this?

Read Hebrews 4:12-13

9. Does Hebrews 4:12-13 describe the sword as being a weapon against the enemy or an instrument of spiritual growth? How is the Word of God like a sword as it relates to individual Christians? Have you ever had an experience where God's Word revealed something deep within your life that you did not previously realize was there?
10. Have you ever considered the "sword of the Spirit" being anything other than your leather bound Bible? What is your reaction to the Greek term for "word" being *rhema* and not *logos*? What implications does that have in your life?
11. Tim said, "We must be sensitive to where God is working so we can make significant Kingdom advances with the wonderful message of the gospel. Such effectiveness calls for a prepared church, but it also calls for a listening church." What can Christians do in order to become a listening church?

Digging Deeper:

Read 2 Corinthians 10:3-5

1. Paul described our spiritual weapons by saying they are "not of the flesh, but divinely powerful for the destruction of fortresses." How would you describe our spiritual weapons?
2. This scripture also talks about strongholds or fortresses. What does *fortress* mean? Are there group members who have overcome a stronghold in their lives who would like to share with the group? How do you "take every thought captive?"
3. It is possible that individuals in your group have been deceived into thinking they are Christians, but true salvation has never been experienced. Is there anyone present in the group now who questions the authenticity of their faith? How might your group help individuals who are questioning their salvation?
4. Do you believe that God still speaks today? Does it make you feel a little awkward or hesitant when you hear someone say that God spoke to them? Are you doubtful at first?
5. Have you ever had an experience where you believe God spoke to you? What was it like? How do you know it was God? Is it possible for someone to think God spoke to them, but in fact the voice they heard was not God? How would you know the difference?

Session Six – Chapters Eleven and Twelve

Read Ephesians 6:18-20

1. While technically prayer is not one of the pieces of spiritual armor, Paul chose to end his discussion on spiritual warfare and the needed spiritual armor with a brief call to prayer. How is prayer used in relationship to spiritual armor?
2. Tim quoted Dallas Willard: "The 'open secret' of many 'Bible believing' churches is that a vanishingly small percentage of those talking about prayer and Bible reading are actually doing what they are talking about." Do you agree with Dr. Willard? Have you experienced that reality before in your own life?
3. Tim draws the distinction of prayer sharpening our view of the Kingdom of God in contrast to the darkness of our world. Do you see any correlations to the spiritual weakness of the church today and the prayerlessness exhibited by many Christians? Do other Christians make similar connections? Why do we remain prayerless?

Read Ephesians 6:18 again.

4. What does God mean when He tells us to "pray in the Spirit?" Have you ever prayed in the Spirit? Have you ever prayed but not done so in the Spirit? What was the difference?
5. As intercessors (praying for others), what are some specific things we ought to be praying for one another as we move toward the return of Christ?
6. Tim wrote about the importance of the prayer of praise as it relates to spiritual warfare. Do you find this kind of prayer to be a normal part of your prayer life? What is the significance of praise in relationship to spiritual warfare?

7. What is the role of worship in spiritual warfare in the last days? What is the evidence that Satan is working hard to keep the church from being a worshipping church in these days? What can the church do to experience biblical worship during times of spiritual conflict?
8. Do you agree with Tim's statement when he said, "The first place the battle begins will be consistent across the board for every Christian. The battlefield of which I am speaking is the battlefield of the mind." What is the evidence that this statement is true? How have you seen Satan attack on the battlefield of the mind in our culture today?

Read Romans 12:1-2

9. What are some ways we can prepare our mind for this initial onslaught? What are ways that Satan is attacking our minds through secular philosophies of our day? How can we win this battle?
10. Many people seem to believe that other people are the enemy (spouse, neighbor, boss, etc.). What did Tim mean when he said another battlefield is our relationships?
11. In the remaining part of Chapter Twelve, Tim wrote of specific application for each piece of armor using exploratory questions for the reader. What are some specific things a Christian should do to put on each piece of the spiritual armor?
12. Now that this study is completed, what specific steps are you taking to apply the principles of this book in preparing to stand firm in the last days?

Digging Deeper:

1. Tim said, "We could easily define prayer as conversation with God, but our definition must go deeper. While prayer is an act, it is also a life." What did he mean?

Read Psalm 51:1-10

2. Discuss what a true prayer of repentance would be like for a Christian today. What does repentance mean?
3. How does prayer help Christians to stay alert during times of great spiritual conflict? What implications does being alert have to being on the defense and offense in spiritual warfare?
4. When Paul said to pray with all prayer, what did he mean? Discuss the different ways we pray. Would you agree that many Christians specialize in the "asking" type of prayer? How does this imbalance make a Christian weak in spiritual warfare?

Read 1 Peter 3:15

5. Do you think Christians are ready to "make a defense" for their faith to those who ask? Why or why not? What should we be doing in order to be obedient to this scriptural command?
6. Tim talked about a plan for personal growth. What are some specific things you are doing to put this principle into application in your life?

NOTES

Introduction:

1. History.com Staff, "Stonewall Jackson," *History,com*, 2009, http://www.history.com/topics/stonewall-jackson (accessed on January 18, 2013).
2. "Stonewall Jackson," *Wikipedia*, http://en.wikipedia.org/Wiki/Stonewall_Jackson (accessed on January 18, 2013).
3. Jim Loy, *When An Irresistible Force Meets An Immovable Object*, http://www.jimloy.com/logic/force.htm (accessed on August 19, 2013).
4. Tim LaHaye and Jerry B. Jenkins, *Are We Living In The End Times? (*Carol Stream, Illinois, Tyndale House Publishers, 1999), 3.
5. Grant Jeffrey, *Jesus: The Great Debate* (Nashville, Tennessee, Word Publishing, 1999), 229.
6. First Thessalonians 4:16 – 18 tells us of Christ's return to take Christians away. We call this the rapture. Matthew 24 deals with what seems to be a different return, and Christians often refer to this as the "Second Coming" or the "Glorious Appearing" (Titus 2:13). Zechariah 14:4 indicates Christ will actually touch the earth again at the Mt. of Olives. This is distinguished from the rapture of the church where the church will "meet the Lord in the air."
7. Michael Youssef, *Biblical Literacy: The Antidote to Postmodernism,* http://www.christianity. com/theology/angels-demons-satan/biblical-literacy-the-perfect-antidote-to-postmodernism-11569596,html (accessed on February 8, 2013).

Chapter One

1. Jake Miller, "States Petition to Secede from Union," *CBS News*, November 12, 2012, http://www.cbsnews.com/8301-250_162-57548572/states-petition-to-secede-from-union (accessed February 8, 2013).
2. David Martosko, "White House 'Secede' Petitions Reach 675,000 Signatures, 50-State Participation," *The Daily* Caller, http://dailycaller.com/2012/11/14/white-house-secede-petitions-reach-660000-signatures-50-state-participation (accessed February 8, 2013).

3. Infoplease, "Deadliest Earthquakes on Record," http://www.infoplease.com/ipa/A0884804.html (accessed on August 31, 2013).
4. Adam Miller, "Experts Say Natural Disaster to Increase," *The StarPhoenix*, June 24, 2013 http://www.thestarphoenix.com/news/Experts+natural+disasters+increase/8568612/ story.html (accessed August 31, 2013).
5. Jessica Derschowitz, "Miley Cyrus' VMA performance blasted by Parents Television Council," *CBS News*, August 27, 2013, http://www.cbsnews.com/8301-207_162-57600224/miley-cyrus-vma-performance-blasted-by-parents-television-council (accessed on August 31, 2013).
6. "Same-sex Marriage in the United States," *Cable News Network*, 14, October, 2014, http://www.cnn.com/interactive/us/map-same-sex-marriage (accessed on October 14, 2014).
7. Annie Lowry, "Gay Marriages Get Recognition From the I.R.S.," *The New York Times*, August 29, 2013, http://www.nytimes.com/2013/08/30/us/politics/irs-to-recognize-all-gay-marriages-regardless-of-state.html?_r=0 (accessed on August 31, 2013).
8. Associated Press, "Surge in gun sales creates arms shortage for Austin-area law enforcement," *Dallas News*, http://www.dallasnews.com/news/state/headlines/20130126-surge-in-gun-sales-creates-arms-shortage-for-austin-area-law-enforcement.ece (accessed January 24, 2013).
9. Helena Smith, "Greece lies bankrupt, humiliated and ablaze: is cradle of democracy finished?" *The Guardian*, February 13, 2012, http://www.theguardian.com/world/2012/feb/13/greece-bankrupt-ablaze-cradle-democracy (accessed on August 31, 2013).
10. "Americans Leaving US In Record Numbers," RT, http://rt.com/usa/news/leaving-us-america-country-289 (accessed February 10, 2013).
11. Dylan Griffiths, *Americans Giving Up Passports Jump Sixfold as Tougher Rules Loom*, "Bloomberg News," http://www.businessweek.com/news/2013-08-09/americans-giving-up-passports-jump-sixfold-as-tougher-rules-loom, August 9, 2013 (accessed on August 31, 2013).
12. Danielle Kurtzleben, "National Debt Interest Payments Dwarf Other Government Spending," US News, http://www.usnews.com/news/articles/2012/11/19/how-the-nations-interest-spending-stacks-up (accessed February 10, 2013).
13. NBC News/Wall Street Journal Poll, http://s.wsj.net/public/resources/documents/WSJ_NBCPoll_092408.pdf (accessed on February 6, 2013).

14. Star-Ledger Editorial Board, "Is America In Decline?" NJ.com, Powered by The Star Ledger, http://www.nj.com/njvoices/index.ssf/2012/12/is_america_in_decline_editoria.html (accessed on January 27, 2013).
15. All the World Economies in Trouble One Way or Another," *The International Forecaster*, http://theinternationalforecaster.com/International_Forecaster_Weekly/All_The_World_Economies_In_Trouble_One_Way_Or_Another (accessed on February 10, 2013).
16. Jane Henderson, "As World Spins Faster Toward Trouble, Gore Claims Optimism" *St. Louis Post-Dispatch*, http://www.stltoday.com/entertainment/books-and-literature/as-world-spins-faster-toward-trouble-gore-claims-optimism/article_d6e459d7-5d7c-578a-b8a4-2bf5d61098be.html (accessed on February 12, 2013).
17. Various passages point to the Antichrist in the Bible. 1 John 2:18 is one of those passages. In other passages he is called "the lawless one" (2 Thessalonians 2:8), the "Beast" (Revelation 11:7), and the "Son of Perdition" (2 Thessalonians 2:3).
18. "Braxton Hicks or True Labor Contractions?, *WebMD Medical Reference*, http://www.webmd.com/baby/guide/true-false-labor (accessed on February 15, 2013).

Chapter Two

1. Albert E. Brumley, *This World Is Not My Home*, Albert E. Brumley and Sons, Clearbox Rights, Brentwood, Tennessee.
2. Elwell, W. A., & Beitzel, B. J. (1988).*Baker Encyclopedia of the Bible* (Grand Rapids, MI: Baker Book House).
3. Rebecca Brooks Gruver, *An American History* (Reading, Massachusetts, Addison-Wesley Publishing Company, 1981), 642.
4. Devvy Kidd, WND Commentary, accessed on February 20, 2013, http://www.wnd.com /2005/06/30874/.
5. The Club of Rome, accessed on April 12, 2013, http://www.clubofrome.org/?p=319.
6. Ibid.
7. Green Agenda, accessed on February 20, 2013, http://www.green-agenda.com/globalrevolution.html.
8. "Case I: The 10 Regions (Unions,Communities, Kingdoms)," *His2nd Coming.Org. Are You Ready?* accessed on February 21, 2013, http://www.his2ndcoming.org/joomla/index.php?option=com_content&task=view&id=58&Itemid=66.
9. David Jeremiah, *What In The World Is Going On? 10 Prophetic Clues You Cannot Afford to Ignore* (Nashville, Tennessee, Thomas Nelson, 2008), 61.

10. George Soros, "No alternative to a new world architecture," *The Japan Times*, November 8, 2009, accessed on January 16, 2013, http://www.japantimes.co.jp/opinion/2009/11/08/commentary/no-alternative-to-a-new-world-architecture/#.UWMgGZ3D_IU.
11. Pete Papaherakles , "Soros Convenes 'Bretton Woods II," *American Free Press*, April 18, 2011, accessed on January 15, 2013, http://www.americanfreepress.net/html/bretton_woods_ii_265.html.
12. "Iran Drops Dollar From Oil Deals," *American Free* Press, December 8, 2007, accessed January 15, 2013, http://afp.google.com/article/ALeqM5jGC7KSKjsKYUTGAF1oR04-yOpBgg.
13. Christopher Doran, "Iran and the Petrodollar Threat to U. S. Empire," *New Left Project*, Accessed January 15, 2013, http://www.newleftproject.org/index.php/site/article_comments/iran_and_the_petrodollar_threat_to_u.s._empire.
14. "Heaven's Gate cult members found dead," *History*, March 26, 1997, accessed on April 12, 2012, http://www.history.com/this-day-in-history/heavens-gate-cult-members-found-dead.
15. John Zarrella and Patrick Oppmann, "Pastor with 666 tattoo claims to be divine," *CNN.com*, February 19, 2007, accessed on April 11, 2012, http://www.cnn.com/2007/US/02/16/miami.preacher.
16. Richard Lacayo, "The Lure of the Cult," *Time*, April 7, 1997, 45.
17. Tim LaHaye and Jerry Jenkins, *Are We Living In the End Times?*(Carol Stream, IL: Tyndale House, 2011), 38.
18. Ibid., 42.
19. USGS Science for a Changing World, *Earthquake Facts and Statistics*, accessed on September 10, 2013, http://earthquake.usgs.gov/earthquakes/eqarchives/year/eqstats.php.
20. "Gospel Spread in Last Days: Wycliff Bible Translators," *Prophecy In The* News, accessed on January 10, 2013, http://prophecynewsdaily.com/article/29/pg/1/Gospel_Spread_in_Last_Days.html.
21. Michael Roy and Scott MacGregor, "The Signs of the End," accessed on July 25, 2013, http://thesignsoftheend.wordpress.com/2013/03/26/the-future-foretold.

Chapter Three

1. Joel C. Rosenberg, *Implosion – Can America Recover From Its Economic and Spiritual Challenges in Time?* (Carol Stream, Illinois, Tyndale House Publishers, 2012), 103-104.
2. John MacArthur, *The Second Coming* (Wheaton, Illinois, Crossway, 1999), 51.

3. Ryan Mauro, "Iran Boasts of End to US-Israeli Alliance," *Frontpage Mag, May 16, 2012,* accessed on September 4, 2013, http://frontpagemag.com/2012/ryan-mauro/iran-boasts-of-end-to-us-israeli-alliance/.
4. John Ortberg, *The Life You've Always Wanted* (Grand Rapids, Michigan, Zondervan, 1997), 41-58.

Chapter Four

1. Peter Wagner, *The Third Wave of the Holy Spirit: Encountering the Power of Signs and Wonders Today*, (Ann Arbor, Michigan, Servant Publishers, 1988).
2. Peter Wagner, *Signs and Wonders Today* (Lake Mary, Florida, Creation House, 1987).
3. Jerry Gardner, *Spiritual Warfare: A Study in Contemporary Thought*; http://www.wrs.edu/Materials_for_Web_Site/Journals/5-1%20Feb-1998/Gardner%20-%20Spiritual%20Warfare.pdf.
4. Bob Sjogren, Bil Stearns, Amy Stearns, *Run With the Vision* (Minneapolis, Minnesota, Bethany House Publishers, 1995), 43-45.
5. Bill Gillham, *Lifetime Guarantee: Making Your Christian Life Work and What to Do When It Doesn't* (Eugene, Oregon, Harvest House Publishers, 1993), 82.
6. Ibid, 97.
7. Hebrews 12:1-2.

Chapter Five

1. Rick Renner, *Dressed to Kill: A Biblical Approach to Spiritual Warfare and Armor*, Kindle Edition (Tulsa, Oklahoma, Harrison House Publishers, 2012), Kindle Location 2691.
2. Dictionary.com, http://dictionary.reference.com/browse/sound?s=t.
3. George Barna, "Barna Survey Examines Changes in Worldview Among Christians over the Past 13 Years," *Barna Group*, accessed on August 12, 2013, https://www.barna.org/barna-update/article/21-transformation/252-barna-survey-examines-changes-in-worldview-among-christians-over-the-past-13-years#.UjBxrp3D9jo.
4. Charles Swindoll, *The Church Awakening: An Urgent Call for Renewal* (New York, Faithwords, 2010), xv.
5. Barack Obama, *The Audacity of Hope: Thoughts on Reclaiming the American Dream* (New York, Random House Publishers, 2006), 93.

6. American Originals, *Washington's Inaugural Address*, accessed on March 12, 2013, http://www.archives.gov/exhibits/american_originals/inaugtxt.html.
7. "Truth-Founders' Quotes," Free Republic, accessed March 12, 2013, http://www.freerepublic.com/focus/f-news/2069062/posts.
8. Nancy Pearcey, *Total Truth: Liberating Christianity from Its Cultural Captivity* (Wheaton, Illinois, Crossway Books, 2004-2005), 19.
9. David Jeremiah, *Living With Confidence in a Chaotic World: What On Earth Should We Do Now?* (Nashville, Thomas Nelson, 2009), 141.

Chapter Six

1. Sam Spencer, *How Big Is The Porn Industry In The United States*, accessed on June 6, 2013, http://www.covenanteyes.com/2012/06/01/how-big-is-the-pornography-industry-in-the-united-states/.
2. Sports Industry Overview, Plunkett Research, accessed on June 6, 2013, http://www.plunkettresearch.com/sports-recreation-leisure-market-research/industry-statistics.
3. Al Krulick, "Bankruptcy Statistics," *Debt.org*, accessed on July 22, 2013, http://www.debt.org/bankruptcy/statistics.
4. I attended the Pastor's Conference in Houston, Texas at the annual meeting of Southern Baptists. Pastor Gregg Matte, of First Baptist Church of Houston, Texas, told the group about his experience with Dr. Billy Graham and shared his concerns about the lostness within our own churches.
5. Dictionary.com, accessed on July 22, 2013, http://dictionary.reference.com/browse/offer?s=t.

Chapter Seven

1. Lauren Axelrod, "Hattusha (Hattusa) Archeological Site In Bogazkoy Turkey," *Ancient* Digger, accessed August 12, 2013, http://www.ancientdigger.com/2010/08/hattusha-hattusa-archaeological-site-in.html.
2. Tim LaHaye and Jerry B. Jenkins, *Are We Living In The End Times? Current Events Foretold In Scripture…And What They Mean* (Carol Stream, Illinois, Tyndale House Publishers, 1999), 3.
3. Cornelius Plantinga, *Not The Way It's Supposed To Be: A Breviary Of Sin*, (Grand Rapids, Michigan, William B. Eerdmans Publishing Company, 1995), 10.
4. Larry Richards, The *Full Armor of God, Defending Your Life From Satan's Schemes* (Bloomington, Minnesota, Chosen Books, 2013), 75.

5. John 17:23 contains the words of Jesus as He prayed for His Church. His request is for our unity, and He states that it is the unity of the Church that will lead people to see that Jesus is indeed the Messiah sent by God.
6. Bishop John Shelby Spong, *Why Christianity Must Change or Die* (San Francisco, CA, HarperCollins Publishers, 1999).
7. David Platt, *Radical* (Colorado Springs, Colorado, Multnomah Books, 2010), 141.
8. Thom Rainer, *The Unchurched Next Door* (Grand Rapids, Michigan, Zondervan, 2003), 24.
9. C. S. Lewis, *Mere Christianity* (San Francisco, CA, HarperCollins Publishers, 1980), 199.

Chapter Eight

1. David Jeremiah, *What In The World Is Going On*, (Nashville, Tennessee, Thomas Nelson, 2008), 66.
2. Joseph Henry Thayer, quoted in Kenneth S. Wuest, (1997). *Wuest's word studies from the Greek New Testament: for the English reader* (Eph 6:12). Grand Rapids: Eerdmans.
3. Kenneth S. Wuest, *Wuest's word studies from the Greek New Testament: for the English reader* (Grand Rapids: Eerdmans, 1997).
4. Dan Williams, "Israel's Netanyahu Says Iran Closer to Nuclear 'Red Line", *Reuters Edition*, July 14, 2013, accessed August 2, 2013, http://news.yahoo.com/israels-netanyahu-says-iran-closer-nuclear-red-line-164208586.html.
5. Ibid.
6. The London Times, Vladimir Putin pledges to complete Iranian nuclear reactor, *The London Times*, October 17, 2011, accessed on November 1, 2011, http://www.timesonline.co.uk/tol/news/world/middle_east/article2673546.ece.
7. David L. Phillips, "Bashir's Sudan and Iran: An Alliance of Terror," *The Sudan Tribune*, January 11, 2013, accessed on January 25, 2013, http://www.sudantribune.com/Sudan-Iran-sign-military,26294.
8. "Early Thermal Weapons," Wikipedia, accessed on April 18, 2013, http://en.wikipedia.org/wiki/Early_thermal_weapons.
9. Wikianswers, accessed on April 22, 2013, http://wiki.answers.com/q/Why_do_lions_roar.
10. I attended the Pastor's Conference in Jacksonville, Florida in January of 2013 where I heard Dr. Preston Nix speak. Dr. Nix is the Professor of

Evangelism and Evangelistic Preaching at New Orleans Baptist Theological Seminary in New Orleans, Louisiana.
11. J. Goldman, M. K. Salus, D. Wolcott, and k. Y. Kennedy, "A Coordinated Response to Child Abuse and Neglect: The Foundation for Practice," *Child Welfare Infomration* Gateway, 2003, accessed on January 18, 2013, https://www.childwelfare.gov/pubs/usermanuals/foundation/foundatione.cfm.
12. Rick Renner, *Dressed to Kill: A Biblical Approach to Spiritual Warfare and Armor* (Tulsa, Oklahoma: Harrison House Publishers, 2007), Kindle Edition – 3608.
13. Dictionary.com, accessed on October 23, 2012, http://dictionary.reference.com/browse/sovereign?s=t.
14. Hillary Whilte, "Christians Are the Most Persecuted Group in the World, Expert Says," *Lifesite News*, May 31, 2013, accessed on June 13, 2013, http://www.lifesitenews.com/news/christians-are-the-most-persecuted-group-in-the-world-expert-says.
15. Stephen Argue, "From Faith to Faithing: Could Faith be a Verb?," Stickyfaith, accessed on April 2, 2013, http://stickyfaith.org/articles/from-faith-to-faithing.

Chapter Nine

1. David Jeremiah, *What in the World is Going On*, (Nashville, TN: Thomas Nelson, 2008), 65.
2. While I do not know who to credit with the overall concept of the three tenses of salvation, I must say that early in my life, I heard this teaching that I see taught throughout the scripture.
3. 1 Thessalonians 4:16-18 tells of Christ's return to meet His church in the clouds.

Chapter Ten

1. Renner, Rick, *Dressed to Kill: A Biblical Approach to Spiritual Warfare and Armor* (Tulsa, Oklahoma: Harrison House Publishers, 2012), Kindle Edition, Kindle Location 4222.
2. "History of Roman Swords," *Sword History*, accessed on June 12, 2013 http://www.swordhistory.info/?p=120.
3. Lemke, S. W., Logos. (C. Brand, C. Draper, A. England, S. Bond, E. R. Clendenen, & T. C. Butler, Eds.) *Holman Illustrated Bible Dictionary* (Nashville, TN: Holman Bible Publishers, 2003).
4. Henry Blackaby, *Experiencing God: Knowing and Doing the Will of God* (Nashville, TN: Lifeway Press, 2009), 90.

5. Dallas Willard, *Hearing God: Developing a Conversational Relationship with God* (Downers Grove, IL: Intervarsity Press, 1999), 9.

Chapter Eleven

1. John Novak, *Don't Worry About It,* Active Rain, http://activerain.com/blogsview/30070/don-t-worry-about-it- (accessed on November 1, 2011).
2. Dorothy Neddermeyer, Worry – A State of Mind – Tips to Stop, http://ezinearticles.com/?Worry---A-State-Of-Mind---Tips-To-Stop&id=6414432 (accessed on May 8, 2013).
3. "Post-ABC Poll," *The Washington Post,* December, 2012, http://www.washingtonpost.com/page/2010-2019/WashingtonPost/2012/12/24/National-Politics/Polling/release_189.xml (accessed on May 8, 2013).
4. David Ropeik, "Worry…A lot…That So Many of Us Are Worried," *Big Think,* 8 January, 2013, http://bigthink.com/risk-reason-and-reality/worrya-lotthat-so-many-of-us-are-so-worried (accessed on February 8, 2013).
5. Dallas Willard, *Spirit of the Disciplines* (San Francisco, HarperSanFrancisco, a division of Harper Collins Publishers, 1988), 186.
6. Ibid., 69.
7. Richard Foster, *Prayer: Finding The Heart's True Home* (New York, HarperCollins Publisher, 2002), 3.
8. Willard, 156.
9. T. W. Hunt, *The Doctrine of Prayer* (Nashville, Tennessee, Convention Press, 1986) 46.
10. Karl Menninger, *Whatever Became of Sin* (Portland, OR: Hawthorne Books, 1973).
11. Vincent, M. R., *Word studies in the New Testament* (Vol. 1, p. 224). (New York: Charles Scribner's Sons, 1887).
12. Blackaby, 84.
13. K. S. Wuest, *Wuest's word studies from the Greek New Testament: for the English Reader*, (Grand Rapids: Eerdmans, 1997).

Chapter Twelve

1. "American's Reading Habits Over Time," *Pew Research* Center, June 25, 2013, http://www.pewresearch.org/2013/06/25/library-readers-book-type/ (accessed on August 2, 2013).
2. Brooks Richey, "Why Are Teens Leaving the Faith," *Lifeway,* http://www.brooksrichey.com/about-book/ (accessed on July 5, 2013).

3. Brian Housman, "Why Are Teens Leaving the Faith," *Lifeway*, June 17, 2013, http://www.lifeway.com/Article/ministry-family-Why-are-Teens-Leaving-the-Faith (accessed on July 18, 2013).
4. "Systematic Theology," *Wikipedia*, http://en.wikipedia.org/wiki/Systematic_theology, accessed on May 5, 2013.
5. Norman Geisler, *Systematic Theology: In One Volume* (Grand Rapids, Michigan: Bethany House, 2011).
6. Norman Geisler, *Systematic Theology: In One Volume* (Grand Rapids, Michigan: Bethany House, 2011).
7. D. Martin-Lloyd Jones, *Great Doctrines of the Bible: God the Father, God the Son, God the Holy Spirit, the Church, and the Last Things* (Wheaton, Illinois: Crossway Books, 2012).
8. Millard Erickson, *Christian Theology* (Grand Rapids, Michigan: Baker Academic, 2013).
9. Bill Hybels and Mark Mittelburg, *Becoming A Contagious Christian* (Grand Rapids, Michigan: Zondervan Publishing House, 1994), 156-159.

Other Publications from GreenTree Publishers

Songs from the Heart: Meeting with God in the Psalms is a Bible study/devotional on one of the most loved books of the Bible: the Psalms. Join Dr. Tim Riordan as he shares insights on these beloved passages through Bible teaching and storytelling, making personal application to your life. This book is available in paperback and Kindle e-book format on Amazon.

Dive into an adventure of scuba diving, treasure hunting, danger and suspense in Judah Knight's exciting novel, *The Long Way Home.* When Meg was stranded in the Caribbean, her life was dramatically changed through an encounter with an old friend that turned into adventure, danger, discovery, and love. Meg Freeman and Jon Davenport had experienced the sorrow of losing a spouse, but they found true friendship as they joined together to search for treasure, which ended up being more than gold. Join this couple's adventure of romance and suspense where a simple lift turned into a ride they would never forget. Enjoy Judah Knight's flinch-free fiction that is safe for the whole family. Available in paperback and Kindle e-book on Amazon. The sequel to *The Long Way Home* will be available Spring of 2015.

For more information, visit www.greentreepublishers.com